PYTHON PROGRAMMING

The ultimate guide to learn Python
language fundamentals, tips, tricks, and
excercises in a simple crash course.

Reilly Lutz

Introduction

Python is a high-level programming language that was initially designed in 1991 by Guido Van Rossum and later on developed by Python Software Foundation. This foundation is a non-profit organization launched in March 2001 that holds the intellectual property rights of Python programming language. Programming with Python is super simple and easy due to its syntax the programmers are able enough to express concepts in fewer lines of code. Even a new learner can easily learn Python language without facing any problems.

The advancement of technology is mainly due to human-computer interactions. For this interaction, different programming languages have been built over the years that usually refer to high-level languages. Humans use high-level languages due to readability with which humans have made excellent achievements. Low-level language refers to machine codes that are machine-readable only. It is difficult for humans to read and understand the low-level language that is why it was felt necessary to develop high-level languages in order to create multiple ways for human-computer interactions. The high-level languages are easy to write and compile. Nowadays, it is common to see multiple options of the programming languages among which Python language has become a favorite choice of programmers. The Python language can be applied to any computer program regardless of considering the operating system such as Windows, Linux, and

Mac, etc. In comparison with other programming languages, no need to change the Python codes for a different operating system but it is a significant disadvantage when it comes to other programming languages such as C, C++, and Java, etc. Due to many reasons, Python is preferred and widely used for computer programming.

Since 2003, Python programming language ranked in the top 10 programming languages and has been improving consistently from version to version. According to statistics, Python is counted as one of the top 5 programming languages to learn in 2019. It has become an essential part of the programming community due to its flexibility, simplicity, easiness, robustness, speed, versatility, and compatibility. Furthermore, technology giants like Google base, Spotify, and Instagram require architectures in Python. In short, Python programming language has become the central figure of the business and programming world. The reasons for its importance are many, but the Python offers the best security and scalability due to which a considerable portion of the business and financial sectors give it the first approach.

Getting started with Python is the same as learning other programming languages, but the codes are different. Learning to Python is like learning any new skill. There is an abundance of resources on the internet related to Python training and learning that creates confusion for learners to pick the right choice. In this learning guide to Python, learners will be enriched with the key concepts and knowledge to get hands-on the basics and then upgrade to the advanced level. The introduction gives you a solid foundation in the basics and opens up into advanced level. It will not be an exaggeration to consider that the reason behind the success of today's programmers and the advanced technologies is the Python programming language.

Why Python?

Python language is preferred due to its unique and advanced features. Some of them are discussed below.

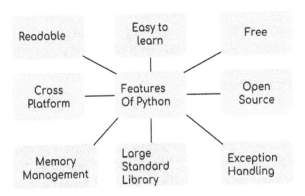

Readability: Python is the most readable language among all the high-level programming languages. The syntax allows programmers to express huge concepts in fewer lines of code. Due to its readability, Python is the best choice of today's programmers.

Easy to Learn: The Python language is easy to learn and compile even new programmers or beginners can easily learn it without facing any problem, but learning the basic structure and concepts is a must thing.

Open Source: Python language is an open-source programming language. Other communities are also built for the interaction of programmers in different open-source projects related to Python programming language.

Cross-Platform: Python can run on all the operating systems such as Windows, Linux, and Mac, etc. Unlike other programming languages, it is not necessary to change Python codes for different operating systems. Simply install the software and run your codes.

Large Standard Library: It contains large standard libraries including functions and some handy codes which can be used to get rid of lengthy codes. A programmer can create a self-built function according to the work they need to perform.

Free Use: Python is available for free download and use. A programmer can download the Python software free of cost and can use it for long life development. Its source code is available, and one can modify the code since it is open-source software and its copies can be distributed freely.

Advanced Features: Python has many advanced features that make it better than all the other programming languages. The advanced features can be found in Python only such as generators, iterators, and decorators, etc.

Exception Handling: Exceptions may exist in the code of a programmer but no need to worry, Python supports exception handling that enables a programmer to test codes for exceptions that may happen later. Due to exceptions, a program can crash anytime, and all the codes can appear in front of users that is also a failure and could be dangerous. Your program can either crashes or can disrupt the normal flow of the program. Using Python exception handling feature, a programmer can write less error-prone code with which various scenarios can be tested, and exceptions can be handled.

Automatic Memory Management: No need to clear or free memories before writing new functions and other handy codes because Python supports automatic memory management that replaces the previous memories with new codes that need to be stored.

What are the applications of Python?

Applications of the Python language are amazing and impressive. Almost all the latest technologies have been built by using Python language. Here are some applications which are flashed out and of great importance.

- Website Development
- Machine Learning
- Data Analysis
- Scripting
- Game Development

- Embedded Application Development
- Desktop Applications

Website development: There are many Python web frameworks such as Django web framework (the most popular web framework), Pyramid, Flask, web2py, Grok, and TurboGears web frameworks. With these frameworks, programmers can easily build website applications. These frameworks help you out in writing server-side code, which helps in managing database, mapping URLs, backend programming logics, etc. Python is a favorite language among programmers, and they are happy with the frameworks based on Python. Google, Quora, and YouTube are also built with Python language.

Machine learning: Machine learning in Artificial Intelligence (AI) is of great importance in which Python is mainly used with PyTorch (developed by Facebook) and Tensorflow (developed by Google) etc. There are numerous machine learning applications built with Python, such as for product recommendation in online shops like Amazon, eBay, Flipkart, etc. are all machine learning algorithms that recognize the interest of users. It is actually a way to write logical codes with Python, and then the codes are used by machines to learn and solve problems on their own. Many Python-based AI applications are available for face and voice recognition and can be downloaded for free to your smartphone.

Data Analysis: Python can be used to analyze and visualize data through charts. There are many applications to analyze data both in graphical form and statistical form. The Pandas is a well-known Python library for data analysis, mainly importing data from spreadsheets. A considerable number of spreadsheets can be calculated within seconds by using functions specific to which type of calculation needs to be calculated and analyzed.

Scripting: Scripting is actually writing codes to develop small applications for simple tasks such as sending automated response emails, private messages, etc. Such small applications can also be developed by using Python programming language.

Game development: Games can also be developed using the Python language, and there are lots of Python-based game applications available on the internet for free. Programmers are doing exceptionally well in the game development side by writing huge concepts into fewer lines of code.

Embedded application development: Python language is used in developing embedded systems like any other programming language. Most of the embedded applications are developed by using C, C++ languages, but nowadays, Python is preferred due to its readability and writing ability.

Desktop applications: In desktop applications, Python language can be used, and almost all the programmers are using Python language to develop desktop applications. The GUI applications allow users to interact with different electronic devices due to its visualization/visual indicators. The importance of these applications is now much more with the use of Python language.

The Evolution of Python Language Over the Years

Python was a hobby project of Guido Van Rossum in 1989. During his office holidays, he decided to work on a project and utilize his time. He named the project as Python and planned to create an interpreter for a new scripting language. The code was released publically in 1991 after he wrote the interpreter successfully. Later on, Python was managed by the Python software foundation.

Version 1 of Python: In 1994, Python of version 1.0 was released. This was the first version of Python with few features and functional programming tools. The tools, including filter, lambda, map, etc. After the first version, version 1.4 was released with several new features including built-in support, keyword arguments, and basic form of data. The major version was upgraded and followed by two minor releases (1.5 and 1.6). The first version of Python had no advanced features, but later on, after a few releases, it was enriched with advanced features. However, the initial version of Python created a strong foundation for the development of a futuristic programming language.

Version 2 of Python: Python of version 2.0 was released on October 2000. This version of Python was released with a garbage collection system and new list comprehension features. The new list comprehension feature was inspired by Haskell and few other programming languages, but unlike

Haskell, the Python 2.0 version had a preference quality. This version gave preference to alphabetic keywords over the punctuation characters. The major release was followed by minor releases with added functionalities and advanced features. The major releases had a number of added functionalities such as nested scopes, and unification of classes and types of Python into a single hierarchy.

Version 3 of Python: Python is considered as the most advanced version released in 2008. The previous version was modified into version 3.0 with several new features and added functionalities and enhancements. It also had deprecated features that proved that this version is completely different from the previous versions. The added features and functionalities, along with the deprecated features, made it a popular and modern version. Most of the developers had been upgraded from old versions to newer ones, but still, many programmers like to use Python 3.0 in order to avail the new awesome features.

In this version, the print statement was replaced by built-in print ( ) function. In this way, the programmers are allowed to use a custom separator between lines. The rules of ordering comparisons were simplified. It raises a TypeError exception if the operands are not organized in a natural way or in a meaningful order. Instead of Unicode and 8-bit strings, the Python programming version 3.0 uses texts and data.

Programmers must be familiar with the APIs and changes made to syntax. As Python version 3.0 is backward incompatible, access to the features like old-styled classes, string exceptions, and implicit relative imports cannot be allowed to programmers. The programmers can use a tool that is called "2to3" to migrate to Python of version 3 from version 2 smoothly. With the help of this tool, the areas that need to be upgraded highlight with warnings and comments. The comments enable programmers to make changes to codes and upgrade the outdated version into the latest version.

The latest version of Python: Developers use Python of version 3.4, which is the latest version but also version 2.7. Version 2.7 has improved numeric handling and enhancements for a standard library that enables programmers to avail them. This version also makes it easier for programmers to migrate to version 3. Besides, Python of version 3.4 came with the most advanced features and added functionalities such as library modules, CPython implementation and improvement, security improvements, and several other new features. However, in both the Python API and programming language, a number of features are deprecated. But the version 3.4 of Python can be used by programmers in the long run.

Version 4 of Python: version 4 of Python has not released yet and is expected to be available by March 2023. After the release of version 3.9 of Python, version 4 of Python will be released with advanced features that will make the process much easier and efficient for programmers. The programmers can easily switch from version 3 to 4. It is not a big issue for the experts and professionals to understand the new versions, but the developers take time to understand the use of newly added functionalities and features.

Version 2, 3 are different: version 2 of the Python language and version 3 of the Python language are completely different from each other. Therefore, a developer must study which version is compatible and best matches the project. In order to select the best choice, a programmer must study the features and functionalities of both versions. After knowing to both the versions, programmers would be able enough to choose the right one for their projects. Also, developers need to check out the versions of Python that each framework supports. However, for long term support, the programmers can take advantage of the latest version of Python to avail all the new features and added functionalities.

Why has Python become an Industry Favorite Among Programmers?

No doubt, Python has become an industry favorite among programmers and developers due to its easiness and contraction of lengthy codes into fewer lines. Python is very useful not only limited to education and computing but also in the data science field and web development. The world is stepping towards a new age of technological advancement, and it is not impossible to envision a future full of screens. For this purpose, the rises in demand of people with excellent programming skills will be required to support and work for further advancement of technology. The popularity of Python language continues to rise with the growing industry and also its use preferred by tech giants like Google, along with NASA and companies belong to social media. However, the significant contributions of Python are discussed below in the advanced fields that make it an all-time better choice.

Getting Innovative: Python language has helped the developers to bring the real world and the computing closer, with its Respberry Pi. Respberry Pi is the name of series single-board computers. It allows developers to access computing education easily.

Respberry Pi:is an inexpensive card-sized microcomputer that helps to build DIY like video games, robots and remote-control cars, etc. Python language is used to powers this micro-computer.

Python has made the life of programmers easier and friction-less. There are many DIY projects available online for practicing and learning.

Machine Learning in AI and Data Science:

The use of Python has been raising over the years, especially in machine learning and data science fields. Data scientists get hands-on projects and prefer to use Python language for friction-less and the most accurate programming results. AI in machine learning is of great importance, and the use of Python has been fastest among the AI aspirants. The "Opportunity Rovers" sent to the Mars planet and the most popular robot "Sophia" are the results of machine learning with Python language. The artificially intelligent robots designed for such big projects have helped scientists to explore more about the universe, and it is of no doubt that Python programming language has the most contributions in such accomplishments.

Large Developer Community: Python programming language has built a vast excited developers community because it is used in numerous applications in AI, productivity tools and video games, etc. There are abundant libraries of Python available that are most likely to help build and solve problems. Nowadays, communities are built like PyLadies is one for gender minorities, and many more that shows interest in coding with Python programming language.

Python language is more flexible than any other language. For example, Java is considered as the best competitive language among all the programming languages due to its fast-interpreted ability, but it takes less time to develop with Python than Java. The errors that are diagnosed can easily be fixed by using the Python language. Furthermore, the user community of Python is very large, and developers who face problems somewhere create a post and get help in seconds to fix any error.

What is Python Web Programming?

Python is one of the best programming languages and is widely used for general purpose.

Though it has been used to perform a variety of tasks ranging from data science and machine learning to robotics (especially AI) and hardware programming, web programming can also be done with Python. Nowadays, programmers give priority to the use of Python language in web programming to build applications more efficiently.

Some essential web frameworks are used to build applications. However, it is also a question for new programmers to understand which framework is better for their projects.

What is a web framework?

A web framework is actually the use of tools and resources to build and manage websites, web applications, and web services. The frameworks work as an abstraction tool that allows reusing the code and makes it easier to develop applications.

Why do we need web development frameworks?
Frameworks make it easier for a developer to develop software and websites. The use of frameworks speed up the development, and hence, the development becomes faster, quicker, and more efficient. Most of the web frameworks are available at cheap costs. A framework has strong security implementations. The most benefits of using frameworks are actually due to the community behind them.

Leading
Python
Web Frameworks
Developers Should Know

For complete development, Django and Pyramid are considered bet choices. For good control and prototyping an app, web2py or Flask has something to offer to your project. For simple minimalist solutions, CherryPy is a must framework. Tornado framework also helps in making thousands of concurrent connections to your application at the same time. Dash is also a web framework that is considered as one of the best choices for analytical applications.

Django:

Django is the most popular framework for web development that is simply defined as "the web framework with advanced features for perfectionists with deadlines." It has built-in features that are allowed for a wide range of web applications such as Chatbots, database applications, GPS solutions, etc.

Django has a philosophy that is called DRY (Do not Repeat Yourself) allows and promotes the reuse of code as well as slicing the code time in half. Its modular architecture allows modification of the code components by enabling the option to allow addition or removal of components as much as needed.

Furthermore, Django framework possesses ORM (Object Relational Mapping). The ORM makes it highly compatible with most of the popular databases, including SQL and Oracle. It has the ability to work with several databases at once.

Django is also an SEO friend framework by reducing the page loading time through different techniques and features like compressing JavaScript and caching templates.

Pyramid:

Pyramid is another framework for web applications which defines itself as "not too small, not too big, and just right." Pyramid has the ability to start small. It allows a programmer to code a solid foundation for specific problem-solving projects and then to scale it up as required. In comparison with Django, Pyramid has the same compatibility with both small and large applications, but in complexity, it is not the same as Django.

Pyramid is an outshine framework with a plugin system which allows programmers to perform whatever is required. More specifically, these plugins help allows for the implementation of multiple solutions/results for a given problem.

Pyramid is ideal for single-file applications, authorization or apps oriented, and flexible authentication.

Conclusion:

For server-side programming, Python has been widely used owing to its capabilities of dynamic website creation. Technology giants like NASA and Google use Python programming language due to its use in fast prototyping and the development of highly scalable web applications.

The Python frameworks make web development friction-less and reduce development efforts. The only challenge for programmers is to identify which framework they need for a specific task or better results.

Important Python Frameworks of the Future for Developers

The professional programmers, also called experts, have explained that according to the needs, benefits, uses, advanced features, and functionalities, programmers would most likely work with few frameworks in the long run. Here are the best frameworks of all time and also favorite for future use:

- CherryPy
- Tornado
- Bottle
- Flask
- CubicWeb

CherryPy:

CherryPy is one of the oldest Python frameworks but still with added functionalities and updated versions it is still most likely used framework. CherryPy is quite stable and fast as compared to other frameworks.

Programmers can build web applications with the help of this framework in a similar way to how they build any other object-oriented application. It results in the development containing smaller source code in less time. Since its launch, CherryPy has shown to be quick enough and efficient.

Features: Following are the major features of CherryPy Python framework:

- CherryPy runs on Python of version 2.7+ and 3.5+, Android, PyPy, and Jython
- It has a flexible and specialized plugin system
- Its powerful configuration system is another feature for developers
- It is super simple and easy to run multiple HTTP servers at once
- CherryPy also offers the testing support, profiling support and built-in coverage in its features
- Its features also include built-in tools for encoding, caching, authentication, sessions, static content, etc.

Tornado:

Tornado is also one of the most popular Python frameworks. It has asynchronous networking library which can be used simultaneously in handling concurrent connections. If the data store or backend takes a long time in processing requests, it helps to do concurrent designs and web services. The concurrent architecture makes it easier for developers to scale designs and keeping the coupling low.

Features: Following are the listed major features of Tornado framework

- Its performance is of high quality
- Developers are allowed to read the source code anytime
- Since it is a small framework, it is best for HTTP+JSON services
- Non-blocking HTTP clients

Bottle:

Bottle is another web framework for the Python programming language. More specifically, it is a WSGI (Web Server Gateway Interface) micro-web framework and is designed in such a way that its use is super simple and its performance is super-fast and of lightweight (50-60 kb). Most interesting about this web framework that it has no dependencies except the Python standard library. It is distributed as a single file module. It allows the development of web applications effectively and quickly.

Features: Bottle web framework has the following main features

- It helps in routing provided that a programmer must use simplified syntax or expressions for URL parameters
- This framework provides convenience to access form data, file uploads, headers, cookies, and other HTTP metadata
- It helps the developers to optimize the speed by testing the fast static routes and frequently used routes.
- It runs with both Python 2.5 and 3.5

Flask:

Flask is a micro web framework for the Python programming language. It does not need particular libraries or tools due to which it is classified as a micro-framework. It is super simple and has no database abstraction layer, form validation, or any pre-existing libraries that provide common functionalities.

Features: Flask web framework has the following features

- It contains development server and debugger
- Extensive documentation can be done
- Provide support for secured cookies

- Provide integrated support for unit testing
- Unicode-based feature

Cubicweb:

CubicWeb is another web framework for Python, which is semantic, open-source web structure, and free. It encourages engineers to construct a web application productively with the help of reusing 3D shapes called segments and by following notable item situated plan standards. For the advancement of a semantic web application, its features are of great importance that includes quality, reusability, and productivity.

Features: CubicWeb has the following main features

- For common needs, a library of reusable components of data model and views is available
- It has a well-developed security workflow
- It supports OWL (Ontology Language) and RDF (Resource Description Framework).

Conclusion:

Many web frameworks for Python have been discussed that give an idea to select and use the one that best matches the project requirements of a programmer. The increase in the usage and development of web applications generally increase the use of such frameworks. Its use depends upon the business requirements and needs in order to decide which Python framework best matches your business. Both online and offline support is available on web services and in many different countries, respectively. These service providers can help programmers to choose the right framework for web development. However, it can also be done if programmers try to explore these web frameworks.

What is Object-Oriented Programming (OOP)?

Object-oriented programming (OOP) is a model in which programs are organized around objects or data without the use of functions and logic. An object has its unique behavior and attributes. In object-oriented programming, the historical approach to programming is opposed while the stress is given to how the logic is written rather than defining the data within the logic. Examples of objects range from physical entities such as humans to small programs like Widgets.

A programmer focuses on the first step known as data modeling in which all the objects are identified to be manipulated, and these objects relate to each other. After identifying an object, then it is generalized as a class of objects. The class defines the kind of data it contains as well as the logical sequence that can manipulate it. Among all the logic sequences, each logic sequence is called a method while the communication of objects with well-defined interfaces is called messages.

In OOP, the developers focus on object manipulation, rather the logic required to manipulate them. This approach is well-suited to programming for the programs, especially the complex, larger, and actively maintained programs. Open-source organizations also support object-oriented programming by allowing programmers to contribute to such projects in groups that results in collaborative development. Furthermore, the additional benefits of object-oriented programming include the code scalability, reusability, and efficiency.

Principles of Object-oriented programming: There are many principles involved in the object-oriented programming. Here are some of them discussed below:

- Encapsulation
- Inheritance
- Abstraction
- Polymorphism

Encapsulation

The state and implementation of each object are held inside a defined class or boundary but privately. Other objects can only access to this class by calling a list of public functions or lists. Else, the objects cannot access to this class or the authority to make changes. Such programming characteristics of data hiding avoid unintended data corruption and provide greater program security.

Inheritance

The object-oriented programming (OOP) ensures a higher level of accuracy and reduces time development. Another property of object-oriented programming results in more thorough data analysis. A relation and subclasses build between the objects which can be assigned and allow developers to reuse a common logic while maintaining the unique hierarchy. This property results in more thorough data analysis, high accuracy, and save time.

Abstraction

The objects reveal the internal mechanisms only. This can be helpful and relevant for the use of other objects. Due to this, the concept of a developer builds that is supportive of going for more addition or making changes over time more easily.

Polymorphism

Depending on the context, objects are allowed to take on more than one form. It is the program that will determine the meaning and usage for each execution of an object, cutting down on the need to duplication code.

Criticism on Object-oriented programming: Developers criticized the object-oriented programming due to multiple reasons. One of the major concerns about object-oriented programming is that it does not focus on computation or algorithms. Object-oriented programming codes may be more complicated to write and take longer to compile. But developers also find alternatives for such complications. The alternatives include the following:

- Functional programming
- Imperative programming
- Structured programming

However, only the most advanced programming languages enable developers with the options to combine them.

Python as an Object-oriented programming language

Python programming language is widely used as an object-oriented programming language for web application development. According to a survey, 90 percent of the programmers prefer to work with Python language over other languages due to a lot of reasons. Its simplicity, readability and easy interfacing are the major reasons for its preference. Python is used in object-oriented programming as well as follows a procedural paradigm; hence the advanced and diverse applications come out with clean and super simple codes.

Application development with Python programming language also requires some frameworks with the help of which application development is easier for developers. The most used frameworks include Django, CherryPy, Pyramid, Flask, Qt, PyGUI, and Kivy, etc. The use of these frameworks is based on the nature and the requirements of individual projects. The assistance is provided by these Python frameworks to build sophisticated applications with minimal efforts and time.

Python is a popular scripting language for many software development processes. Furthermore,

Python can be economically utilized to integrate disparate systems together.

Enter into the Programming World with Python Training

Python training is always an excellent idea for those who wish to become a part of this constantly developing industry. Developers need to have a grasp on this language, which is not only easy to grasp but also emphasis less on the syntax. As a result of such convenience, Python is different from other languages and does not create any trouble for programmers even in the case of making a few mistakes here and there.

Python programmers can branch out to different fields on the basis of Python programming language that provides them a solid foundation. The Python training ensures that programmers can use this useful language in many ways to the best of its capabilities. Programmers, especially those who want to make a career as a software engineer can get hands-on projects provided to find Python live up to their expectations.

What is the best way to learn Python?

It may be a bit challenging for students to learn this language and almost all the students ask a common question "what are the best ways to learn Python?" but those who have decided to embark on the journey of learning Python programming language can easily get Python training by following few necessary steps.

- Stick to it
- Daily practice
- Make notes
- Go interactive
- Take breaks
- Debugging
- Collaborative Work
- Build Something

Stick to it

Beginners can master their programming skills only if they act like a glue stick and practice the code repeatedly. Here are some ways for beginners and intermediates to master the skills of Python programming.

Daily Practice

It is recommended for beginners practice the code on a daily basis in order to have a grasp over a specific task. Divide a task into smaller steps if possible. Consistency is the key to achieving any challenging task, which is the same in learning Python, but real programmers believe in consistency. Even a student with little knowledge can make a commitment to code daily for at least an hour.

Make Notes

After making some progress on the journey as a new programmer, making a note of things is also a good idea. Research says that making notes of the important and urgent works with a hand is beneficial for long-term retention. In the case of becoming a real programmer, this habit is very beneficial. Furthermore, writing code on a paper can also help build the mind of a programmer is also difficult in the beginning, but there are programmers who write codes in their minds. So, it is not a big issue in writing on a paper which will result in friction-less thinking ability. This friction-less thinking ability is required for a programmer to get hands-on big projects in the future.

Go Interactive

Beginners can take help of the IDEs in order to practice the Strings, lists, classes, and dictionaries, etc. Install any IDE for practicing the codes. The most easy and simple IDE is the Jupyter Notebook that comes with Anaconda Navigator. Install Anaconda navigator and run the IDE that is Jupyter Notebook. A window will open in the default browser of a desktop computer or laptop and start practicing the code. Write your code and check the results. Make changes to your code and analyze the results and errors. It is a mental practice and helps a lot in learning.

Take Breaks

It is important to take a break and remind the concepts behind the codes. Practice, along with absorbing the concepts work out. There is a well-known technique called a Pomodoro Technique, which is widely used and can help for learning purpose. Take a break after practicing a task for 25-30 minutes, remind the concepts, and then repeat the process. Exercise is a kind of refreshment when you go for a walk or chat with friends. It is also possible to chat with friends about the concepts that have been learned in the course.

Debugging

Becoming bug bounty hunting is vital in programming languages, especially in Python programming. Getting bugs in the code also happens with professionals' mostly in hard tasks, but this is not always the case. However, professionals were also beginners when their journey started. Embrace the moments and do not frustrate yourself when getting these bugs but hunt them. It is essential to have a methodological approach in order to find out where the things are breaking down when debugging. Make sure each part of the written code works out in the most proper way, and this happens if a programmer starts checking the code from start to end at the end.

When the area is identified where the things are breaking down then insert these lines into your code and then press the enter button to run your code. The codes are,

Import pdb; pdb.set_trace( ) ###add the lines to your script and run it

This is the Python debugger while it can also be run with the below line,

Python –m pdb <my_file.py> ###command line

Collaborative Work

Once the programmers are done with sticking to the Python in the starting journey then proceeding to a collaborative work makes it easier for programmers to get hands-on some tasks which might be a little bit challenging but a collaborative work makes it easier. In short, when more than one mind starts thinking about a problem, then the problem does not remain a problem anymore. In order to make it collaborative, here are some tips to follow.

Work with other learners

Learning to code is not easy in the start, but it works best when working with other learners. Sharing the tricks and tips make it easier to learn well and proceed forward. There is no need to worry in the case of having no partner or friend with whom you can work in collaboration. There are always multiple options in which the most possible way is either to join any public events organized for learning the purpose, or online peer-to-peer community support is also available for Python learning enthusiasts.

Teach

It is common to hear from teachers "A teacher learns more when teaching to students," is famous among the teaching and learning communities. This is also valid and true when it comes to learning the Python language. Many options are available in order to teach and learn more by understand and solving problems. Teaching through whiteboard is the most common way to it but also writing blog posts about the tips in learning Python if any, problems or mistakes, solving specific errors, recording videos, and useful tricks. Other than this, there is a super simple way to teach by talking or repeating the same things when done. By doing these strategies, the concepts and understandings will solidify as well as point out any error or gaps if any.

Ask Questions

There should be no good or bad concept when learning the programming language. While asking any question, programmer is free to ask anything bad as it is not a common language. The concepts, rules, and results should be learned in any possible way by asking even foolish questions. However, a programmer needs to ensure asking good questions in such a way that the conversation with others goes well in a pleasant way. It also helps in making it possible to have some more conversation next time when needed.

Build Something

Almost all programmers believe that learning programming is easy when solving a simple problem or build something simple. One must learn by building something, is a kind of perception in order to become a real programmer.

Build Anything Small

There are many exercises to solve, which helps in learning Python language in the most possible way. In this way, a programmer gains confidence, which helps in proceeding forward to much more challenging tasks. Follow this way once a programmer is done with learning to the basic data structures such as lists, dictionaries, classes, strings, and functions, etc. It is now the best time to start building something.

A programmer with the basics can proceed to build something simple that is one of the applications of the concepts came after the Python training and learning. Some of the basics tasks to build something are as follow:

- Number guessing game that continues using the "while loop"
- Any simple calculator application or of additional functionalities
- Dice roll simulator
- Poker game

- Price notification service of any currency

Programmers can also come up with new ideas, but only sharp programmers can develop new ideas or tasks to perform with Python. There are thousands of programming projects or tasks for both the beginners and intermediates to practice and master their skills.

Contribute to Open Source

Open source communities have been built which are cooperating in solving problems and learning new skills. In open source communities, codes are available for specific programs that can be built by the programmers who want to practice and master their skills by building something. Many open-source organizations, including both the low-ranked and high-ranked companies as well as mentors, are available and open to help on Github and other platforms. By staying active in such open-source communities, a programmer can get the codes and work with them uploaded by engineers.

Contributing to an open-source project is a great way to bring your knowledge into action. A programmer can submit any bug fix request or can get help in his own script to fix the bugs. By doing so, the managers of the projects leave replies on your posts that might be useful and can be learned. In such a way, a programmer learns more by communication with other developers, especially the experienced ones or may be helpful to other learners is a kind of contribution to the open-source community.

Why is Python a Preferred Language for Startups?

When startups are planning a process of product development, they need to keep in mind and consider multiple factors when it comes to choosing the right language for programming. Moreover, since many startups start from scratch, the budget available is often low, and this is why they very carefully consider factors like how swift the development would be, how popular and widely use the language is factors like the cost of libraries, integrations, and developers. In addition, the cost of security and scalability and not to forget stability. Due to these reasons, it is always preferred by startups around the world and especially in Silicon Valley to opt for a robust and strong technology like Python, which is established and deep-rooted.

This is not the start of technology. It has been around for more than as long as 30 years in the market, and it is so robust and established that it is still one of the tops and best languages for programming that ever existed. This means that Python is so established and widely used that even the latest innovations in the IT sector could not elbow it aside. According to a survey by BuiltWith, as many as one million websites out there are Python costumers and have been performing pretty amazingly with great returns. Credit goes to the robust programing language. Another survey about the popularity of Python by TIOBE INDEX reveals that an index called programming community index PCI that measures how popular the programing languages are has ranked Python as the third most famous and popular programing language around the world.

So, why is Python so popular as a programing language?
This question often pops up in minds.

Python is very dynamic, high level and object-oriented language for programming, and this is exactly what the startups need. It is like you need tomatoes and onions for making an omelet for breakfast. Python actually focuses and concentrates on instant and robust progress and development and could be widely used for projects of diverse sizes. The project size could be as giant as that of Facebook, IBM, Instagram, Google, Spotify, Netflix, and Dropbox, and many more and all of them depend on Python to a great extent. Many other famous and fast-rising startups would never have done it without Python and have it always in the tech stack, and startups like 21Buttons, Festicket, and TravelPerk are the famous examples. Uber is also making use of the programing language.

This means that if you want your startup to evolve into a great company, you have to incorporate Python in your tech stack as we have seen it one of the integral parts of these leading companies around the world.

So the question comes into mind that why these leading companies chose Python as a preferred language for programming. What makes Python a fantastic and attractive programing language for these famous startups and those growing startups?

User Friendly:

The language is user friendly because it is very simple and beautiful in a lucrative manner and this is the reason Python developers like the language. They say that *"there is one and only one best way to get a job done and that is how it should be done"*. This is something the Python Philosophy says. And this philosophy of python is supported by a number of important and core principles like:

- Simple is preferred to complex
- Complex is preferred to Complicated
- Finally, explicit or clear is preferred to implicit of vague

Popular

Popularity matters and this is why we would love to take an autograph of Tom Cruise rather than going for someone like Tiger Woods, on a lighter note!

As we explained that according to TOIBE Index, Python is the third most popular language and the most demanded in the market in the current era of technological improvement and startup-oriented era.

The popularity is reflected in the job market. A survey by Stack Overflow Developer in which more than 90,000 developers participated, elucidates that Python is the fourth most famous and demanded technology and is actually overtaken by SQL and HTML or CSS. This will hit you like a surprise, but Python has been able to surpass Java this year. It was also the second most loved programming language of the year.

Large Community or User Base

Another impressive thing about the fame and popularity of Python is that there is a huge and large number of users and hence supporters out there and in fact, this has made Python's programming community one of its kinds and one of the best in the world. It is only Python with a great, expansive, and devoted and dedicated community.

This means that you would very easily find instant support for any problem you happen to counter during development regardless of the complexity of the problem. There is a huge and infinite number of developers around the globe who are dedicated to improving the core features of the language and its functionalities.

Versatile Nature

Python is the only programing language that could be applied and used in any development scenario. It does not matter if you need code operations for Windows, Linux, or MacOS; Python is the key to do that. It is actually very famous for areas like prototyping, gaming, language programing, web frameworks and while designing graphic designing apps and many more. Python has been impressively in such areas and in addition to it is one of the cores and the main language in data science and Machine Learning ML.

In case your application requires machine learning functionalities, Pythons should be the PL to be considered. Moreover, since it is super simple and high-level language, it is much suitable for fast tweaking for ML algorithms and prototyping and in yet much-preferred language for this type of ventures than the likes of Ruby for example.

Scalable

Finally, you need to have a flexible startup if you want it to grow. However, it is pretty unpredictable when and where would scalability become a priority for the company. So this is the reason it is more than imperative you should choose a programing language that easily can scale up and down. This could also take care of quick growth and maintain it at the same time.

Python 3 Installation & Setup Guide

Python is widely known for its Python 3 installation is few steps away. The latest version of Python is available; however, any release can be downloaded for any operating system. Visit this site **https://www.python.org/downloads/** and select the best downloading option for your operating system. By clicking the link above, you will find a view with multiple options for your download as shown below:

It can be seen that the latest version of Python 3.7.4 is available for download. Click the yellow block if the operating system you are using is windows. If you are using Linix/Unix, then select the option next to the yellow block. Other than the Windows and Linux downloads, downloads are also available for Max OS X and 'other' option includes download for AIX, IBM, and IOS.

Windows

1. Download Python for windows by clicking the yellow block. The file name appears as **python-3.7.4.exe** and its size is about 24.5 MBs.

2. Open the file, a popup window will appear. Click run.

3. A window will appear for installation. Do you want to install Python? Click on install button.

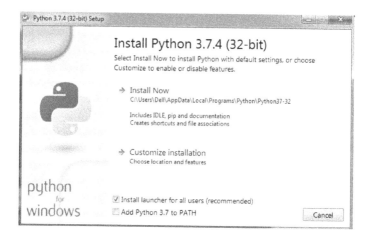

4. It requires an additional 90 MB space of the disk space after installation. So, make sure you select a path with enough free space.

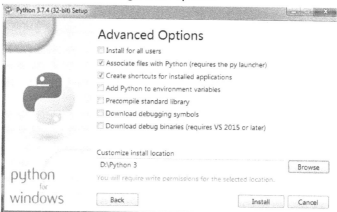

5. After browsing path where the Python will install, click on the install button and installation will start.

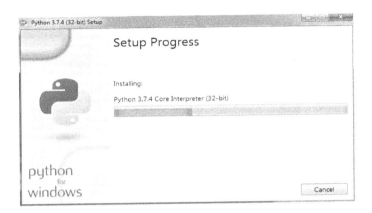

6. The setup completes.

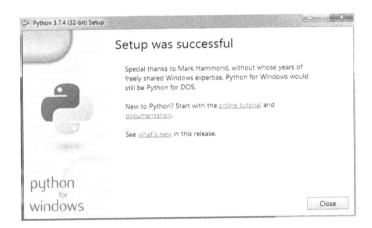

7. Click on the close button.
8. Python is now installed on your PC.

Verifying Process:

Go to your windows applications and open Python. A window will appear as shown below:

Input exit() and then press enter. The setup installation is now verified.

Mac OS X

On Mac OS X, Python is already installed. However, if the already installed software is of Python 2, you can upgrade it to the latest version of Python. Now, visit the same website **https://www.python.org/ downloads/** and download Python for your operating system. Make sure the download is for Mac OS X. Follow the easy steps to install the latest version of Python.

Loops in Python

Loops are used in computer programming, is a sequence of instructions that is used repeatedly for the repetition of a certain code or until any condition is satisfied. Loops are actually controlled structures. There are two types of Python loops (While loop and for-loop). While loop is used to execute code or statement repeatedly until any given condition is satisfied. For loop is used to iterate over any sequence containing items such as strings or lists.

Nested Loops

While and for blocks can contain arbitrary Python statements just like if statements, including other loops (loops inside loops). Nested loops are said to be those loops which contain another loop block. In order to see how the nested loops work, let's take a simple program that prints out a multiplication table. Mostly the elementary school students learn multiplication tables as they learn the products of integers up to 10 or even 12. We are going to create a multiplication table program that should be flexible and allow the user to specify the size of the table. Let's get started with a sample program first. There is no need to worry in the beginning about the printing of the table's row and column titles. Also, there is no need to print the lines separating the titles from the contents of the table. Initially, only the contents of the table will be printed. It will be taken care for using a nested loop to print the table's contents, but that still is too much to manage in our first attempt. In the first attempt, the rows of the table will be printed in a very rudimentary manner. Once our simple program works successfully and satisfies us, then more features can be added. The code below shows the first attempt at a multiplication table.

```
# Get the number of rows and columns in the table
size = int(input("Please enter the table size: "))
# Print a size x size multiplication table
for row in range(1, size + 1):
    print("Row #", row)
```

The output is somewhat underwhelming:

```
Please enter the table size: 10
Row #1
Row #2
Row #3
Row #4
Row #5
Row #6
Row #7
Row #8
Row #9
Row #10
```

The above code does indeed print each row in its proper place. It just does not supply the needed detail for each row. The next step is to refine the way the program prints each row properly. Each row should be of size numbers. It is understandable that each number within each row represents the product of the current row and current column. For example, the number in row 2, column 5 should be 2 × 5 = 10. In each row, therefore, the column number from 1 to size should be varied. The code written code contains the needed refinement.

```python
# Get the number of rows and columns in the table
size = int(input("Please enter the table size: "))
# Print a size x size multiplication table
for row in range(1, size + 1):
    for column in range(1, size + 1):
        product = row*column # Compute product
        print(product, end=' ') # Display product
    print() # Move cursor to next row
```

A loop is used for the purpose of printing the contents of each row. The outer loop controls how many total rows the program prints. On the other hand, the inner loop is executed in its entirety each time the program prints a row as a result when it is possible to print the individual elements that make up a row. The executed result of the above code is as follows:

```
Please enter the table size: 10
1 2 3 4 5 6 7 8  910
2  4 6 8 10 12 14 16 1820
3  6 9 12 15 18  21 24 27 30
4  8 12 16 20 24 28 32 36 40
5 10 15 20 25 30 35 40 45 50
6 12 18 24 30 36 42 48 54 60
714 21 28 35 42 49 56 63 70
8 16 24 32 40 48 56 64 72 80
```

```
9 18 27 36 45 54 63 72 81 90
10 20 30 40 50 60 70 80 90 100
```

It can be seen that the numbers within each column are not lined up nicely, but the numbers are in their correct positions relative to each other from 1 to 10 in the first row and other numbers. We can use the string formatter introduced in order to right justify the numbers within a four-digit area. The code below contains this alignment adjustment.

```python
# Get the number of rows and columns in the table
size = int(input("Please enter the table size: "))
# Print a size x size multiplication table
for row in range(1, size + 1):
    for column in range(1, size + 1):
        product = row*column # Compute product
            print('{0:4}'.format(product), end='') # Display
product
    print() # Move cursor to next row
```

The above code prints the table's contents in an attractive form:

```
Please enter the table size: 10
1   2   3   4   5   6   7   8    9  10
2   4   6   8  10  12  14   16  18 20
3   6   9  12  15  18  21  24  27 30
4   8  12  16  20  24  28  32  36 40
5  10  15  20  25  30  35  40  45 50
6  12  18  24  30  36  42  48  54 60
7  14  21  28  35  42  49  56  63 70
```

```
8   16 24 32 40 48 56 64  72 80
9   18 27 36 45 54 63 72  81 90
10 20 30 40 50 60 70 80 90 100
```

It should be noted that the table presentation adjusts to the user's input:

```
Please enter the table size: 5
1 2 3 4 5
2 4 6 8 10
3 6 9 12 15
4 8 12 16 20
5 10 15 20 25
```

A multiplication table of size 15 can be seen below

```
Please enter the table size: 15
1 2 3 4   5   6   7   8   9 10 11 12 13 14 15
2 4 6 8 10 12 14 16 18 20 22 24 26 28 30
3 6 9 12 15 18 21 24 27 30 33 36 39 42 45
4 8 12 16 20 24 28 32 36 40 44 48 52 56 60
5 10 15 20 25 30 35 40 45 50 55 60 65 70 75
6 12 18 24 30 36 42 48 54 60 66 72 78 84 90
7 14 21 28 35 42 49 56 63 70 77 84 91 98 105
8 16 24 32 40 48 56 64 72 80 88 96 104 112 120
9 18 27 36 45 54 63 72 81 90 99 108 117 126 135
10 20 30 40 50 60 70 80 90 100 110 120 130 140
150
11 22 33 44 55 66 77 88 99 110 121 132 143 154
165
```

```
12 24 36 48 60 72 84 96 108 120 132 144 156 168
180
13 26 39 52 65 78 91 104 117 130 143 156 169 182
195
14 28 42 56 70 84 98 112 126 140 154 168 182 196
210
15 30 45 60 75 90 105 120 135 150 165 180 195 210
225
```

It is needed to add to the row and column titles and the lines that bound the edges of the table. The following list adds the necessary code:

```python
# Get the number of rows and columns in the table
size = int(input("Please enter the table size: "))
# Print a size x size multiplication table
# First, print heading: 1 2 3 4 5 etc.
print(" ", end='')
# Print column heading
for column in range(1, size + 1):
        print('{0:4}'.format(column),  end='')  # Display column number
print() # Go down to the next line
# Print line separator: +------------------
print(" +", end='')
for column in range(1, size + 1):
   print('----', end='') # Display line
print() # Drop down to next line
# Print table contents
for row in range(1, size + 1):
     print('{0:3} |'.format(row), end='') # Print heading for this row
   for column in range(1, size + 1):
```

```
    product = row*column # Compute product
        print('{0:4}'.format(product), end='') # Display
product
    print() # Move cursor to next row
```

When a value 10 supplies, then the above code prints the following:

```
Please enter the table size: 10
1 2 3 4 5 6 7 8 9 10
+--------------------------------------
1 | 1 2 3 4 5 6 7 8 9 10
2 | 2 4 6 8 10 12 14 16 18 20
3 | 3 6 9 12 15 18 21 24 27 30
4 | 4 8 12 16 20 24 28 32 36 40
5 | 5 10 15 20 25 30 35 40 45 50
6 | 6 12 18 24 30 36 42 48 54 60
7 | 7 14 21 28 35 42 49 56 63 70
8 | 8 16 24 32 40 48 56 64 72 80
9 | 9 18 27 36 45 54 63 72 81 90
10 | 10 20 30 40 50 60 70 80 90 100
```

The following is an input of 15 yields:

```
Please enter the table size: 15
1 2 3 4 5 6 7 8 9 10 11 12 13 14 15
+------------------------------------------------------
1 | 1 2 3 4 5 6 7 8 9 10 11 12 13 14 15
2 | 2 4 6 8 10 12 14 16 18 20 22 24 26 28 30
3 | 3 6 9 12 15 18 21 24 27 30 33 36 39 42 45
4 | 4 8 12 16 20 24 28 32 36 40 44 48 52 56 60
5 | 5 10 15 20 25 30 35 40 45 50 55 60 65 70 75
```

```
6 | 6 12 18 24 30 36 42 48 54 60 66 72 78 84 90
7 | 7 14 21 28 35 42 49 56 63 70 77 84 91 98 105
8 | 8 16 24 32 40 48 56 64 72 80 88 96 104 112 120
9 | 9 18 27 36 45 54 63 72 81 90 99 108 117 126 135
10 | 10 20 30 40 50 60 70 80 90 100 110 120 130
140 150
11 | 11 22 33 44 55 66 77 88 99 110 121 132 143 154
165
12 | 12 24 36 48 60 72 84 96 108 120 132 144 156
168 180
13 | 13 26 39 52 65 78 91 104 117 130 143 156 169
182 195
14 | 14 28 42 56 70 84 98 112 126 140 154 168 182
196 210
15 | 15 30 45 60 75 90 105 120 135 150 165 180 195
210 225
```

When the user enters 7, the program prints the following:

```
Please enter the table size: 7
1 2 3 4 5 6 7
+---------------------------
1 | 1 2 3 4 5 6 7
2 | 2 4 6 8 10 12 14
3 | 3 6 9 12 15 18 21
4 | 4 8 12 16 20 24 28
5 | 5 10 15 20 25 30 35
6 | 6 12 18 24 30 36 42
7 | 7 14 21 28 35 42 49
```

The user even can enter a value 1:

```
Please enter the table size: 1
1
+----
1 | 1
```

It can be seen that the table automatically adjusts to the size and spacing required by the user's input.

- It is of great importance to check what is done only once (outside all loops) from that which is done repeatedly. The column heading across the top of the table is outside of all the loops. Therefore, a loop is used by the program to print it one time.

- The work to print the heading for the rows is distributed throughout the execution of the outer loop. This is due to the reason that the heading for a given row cannot be printed until all the results for the previous row have been printed.

- The value of the product is justified by the printing statement rightly in the field that is four characters wide. This technique properly aligns the columns within the times table.

```
print('{0:4}'.format(product), end='') # Display product
```

- The nested loop contains row and column in which row is the control variable for the outer loop while the column controls the inner loop.

- The inner loop executes its size times on the iteration of the outer loop. This means the innermost statement

```
print('{0:4}'.format(product),  end='')  #
Display product
```

Executes size × size times, one time for every product in the table.

- When it displays the contents of each row, the program prints a newline. Thus, all the values printed in the inner (column) loop appear on the same line.

What really necessary is includes the use of nested loops when an iterative process itself must be repeated. In the times table taken as an example, the contents of each row is printed by for loop, and an enclosing for loop prints out each row.

The code below contains a triply-nested loop to print all the different arrangements of the letters A, B, and C. Each string printed is a permutation of ABC. A permutation is actually the possible ordering of a sequence.

```
# File permuteabc.py
# The first letter varies from A to C
for first in 'ABC':
    for second in 'ABC': # The second varies from A to
C
        if second != first: # No duplicate letters allowed
            for third in 'ABC': # The third varies from A to
C
                # Don't duplicate first or second letter
                if third != first and third != second:
                    print(first + second + third)
```

It should be noted that if the statements prevent duplicate letters within a given string, the output of the above code shows all the six permutations:

```
ABC
ACB
BAC
BCA
CAB
CBA
```

The code written below uses a four-deep nested loop in order to print all the different arrangements of the letters A, B, C, and D. Each string printed is a permutation of ABCD.

```python
# File permuteabcd.py
# The first letter varies from A to D
for first in 'ABCD':
    for second in 'ABCD': # The second varies from A to D
        if second != first: # No duplicate letters allowed
            for third in 'ABCD': # The third varies from A to D
                # Don't duplicate first or second letter
                if third != first and third != second:
                    for fourth in 'ABCD': # The fourth varies from A to D
                        if fourth != first and fourth != second and fourth != third:
                            print(first + second + third + fourth)
```

Nested loops are the complex form of using loops which are very powerful and most of the wise programmers use the nested loop to solve the complexities. Before you attempt to solve any problem with a nested loop, it should be noted single loops do not work just like we did above. It is more difficult to write the nested loops correctly, when not necessary, they are less efficient than a simple loop where single loops are useful and can work out.

While/else and for/else

In the Python loops, an optional else block is available. The else block, in the context of a loop, provides code to execute when the loop exits normally. Another possibility, the code in a loop's else block does not work/execute if the loop terminates due to a break statement.

In the case of a loop when exiting due to its condition being false during its normal check then its associated else block executes. The use of else block is cleared now and there should be no further ambiguity. This is true even if its condition is found to be false before its body has had a chance to execute. The code written below shows how the while/else statement works.

```
# Add five nonnegative numbers supplied by the user
count = sum = 0
```

```
print('Please provide five non-negative numbers
when prompted')
while count < 5:
    # Get value from the user
    val = float(input('Enter number: '))
    if val < 0:
            print('Negative numbers not acceptable!
Terminating')
        break
    count += 1
    sum += val
else:
    print('Average =', sum/count)
```

When the user supplies only non-negative values to the above code then it computes the average of the values provided:

```
Please provide five non-negative numbers when
prompted
Enter number: 23
Enter number: 12
Enter number: 14
Enter number: 10
Enter number: 11
Average = 14.0
```

If the case is different in which the user does not comply with the instructions, then the program will print a corrective message and not attempt to compute the average:

```
Please provide five non-negative numbers when
prompted
Enter number: 23
Enter number: 12
Enter number: -4
Negative numbers not acceptable! Terminating
```

It looks more natural to read the else keyword for the while statement as "if no break," meaning execute the code in the else block if the executed code of the program in the while block did not encounter the break statement.

So, the else block is not essential; the code written below uses if/else statement to achieve the same effect as the code written above.

```python
# Add five nonnegative numbers supplied by the user
count = sum = 0
print('Please provide five nonnegative numbers when
prompted')
while count < 5:
    # Get value from the user
    val = float(input('Enter number: '))
    if val < 0:
        break
    count += 1
    sum += val
if count < 5:
        print('Negative numbers not acceptable!
Terminating')
else:
```

```
print('Average =', sum/count)
```

The above-written code uses two distinct Python constructs. The while statement followed by an if/else statement. On the other hand, the previously written code uses only one, a while/else statement. The above code also must check the count < 5 conditions twice, once in the while statement and again in the if/else statement.

The for statement with an else block works in a similar way to the while/else statement. When a for/else loop exits due to the reason that it has considered all the values in its range or all the characters in its string, it executes the code in its associated else blocks. If the case is different and a for/else statement exits prematurely due to a break statement, then it does not execute the code in its else block. The code written below shows how the else block works with a for statement.

```
word = input('Enter text (no X\'s, please): ')
vowel_count = 0
for c in word:
    if c == 'A' or c == 'a' or c == 'E' or c == 'e' \
      or c == 'I' or c == 'i' or c == 'O' or c == 'o':
        print(c, ', ', sep='', end='') # Print the vowel
        vowel_count += 1 # Count the vowel
    elif c == 'X' or c =='x':
        print('X not allowed')
        break
else:
```

```
print(' (', vowel_count, ' vowels)', sep='')
```

The above written code does not print the number of vowels if the user supplies text containing and X or x.

Infinite Loops

When a loop executes its block of statements repeatedly until the user forces the program to quit, such a loop is called an infinite loop. It cannot escape once the program flow enters the loop's body. Infinite loops sometimes in some ways are by design. An example can be taken to remove the ambiguities if any. A long-running server application like a Web server may need to check for incoming connections continuously. The Web server is capable enough to perform checking within a loop that runs indefinitely. Beginners, all too often create infinite loops by accident, and these infinite loops reflect logic errors in their programs. Intentional infinite loops should be made obvious. For example:

```
while True:
    # Do something forever. . .
```

The Boolean literal 'True' is always true, so it is impossible for the condition of loops to be false. The else ways to exit a loop is the break statement, return statement, or a sys.exit call embedded somewhere within its body. Intentional infinite loops are easier to write correctly. Accidental infinite loops are quite common but can be puzzling for beginners to diagnose and repair. Consider the written code below that attempt to print all the integers with their associated factors from 1 to 20.

```python
# List the factors of the integers 1...MAX
MAX = 20 # MAX is 20
n = 1 # Start with 1
while n <= MAX: # Do not go past MAX
    factor = 1 # 1 is a factor of any integer
        print(end=str(n) + ': ') # Which integer are we examining?
    while factor <= n: # Factors are <= the number
        if n % factor == 0: # Test to see if factor is a factor of n
            print(factor, end=' ') # If so, display it
            factor += 1 # Try the next number
    print() # Move to next line for next n
    n += 1
```

It displays:

```
1: 1
2: 1 2
3: 1
```

and "hangs" or "freezes up", ignoring any user input. Behavior of this kind is a frequent symptom of an unintentional infinite loop. The factors of 1 display properly as do the factors of 2. The program hangs after the display of the first factor of 3 properly. As the program is short, then it may be easy to locate the problem. In some programs, the error may be challenging to find. Even in the above-written code, the debugging task is non-trivial as the program involves nested loops. In order to avoid infinite loops, it must be ensured that the loop exhibits certain properties:

The condition of the loop must not be a tautology (a Boolean expression that can never be false). For example, the statement:

```
while i >= 1 or i <= 10:
    # Block of code follows ...
```

would result in an infinite loop as any value chosen for i will satisfy one or both of the two sub-conditions. Perhaps programmer is intended to use and instead of or to stay in the loop as long as it remains in the range 1...10.

In the above code, the outer loop condition is:

n <= MAX

The condition is false when MAX is 20 and n is 21. Since it is possible to find the values for n and MAX that makes this expression false. It cannot be a tautology. Analyzing the inner loop condition:

factor <= n

It can be seen that the expression is false when the factor is 3 and n is 2. Therefore, this expression also is not a tautology.

In order to gain access to the body, the condition of a while must be true initially. The state of the program must be modified by the code in some way so as to influence the outcome of the condition that is checked at iteration. It means that the body must be able enough to modify one of the variables used in the condition. Eventually, the variable assumes a value that makes the condition false due to which the loop terminates.

In the code written and discussed above has the outer loop's condition involves the variables MAX and n. It is observed that 20 is assigned to MAX before the loop and never change it afterward, in order to avoid an infinite loop, it is essential to modify n within the loop. The body of outer loop increments n in the last statement.   Initially, n is 1 and MAX is 20, so unless the situation arises to make the inner loop infinite, then the outer loop should terminate eventually.

The condition of inner loop involves the variables n and factor. There is no such statement in the inner loop that modifies n, so it is imperative that factor is modified in the loop. It is good to see that factor is incremented in the body of the inner loop, but the bad side is that the increment operation is protected within the body of the if statement. The inner loop contains one statement that is the if statement. The statement further contains two statements in its body:

```
while factor <= n:
    if n % factor == 0:
```

```
      print(factor, end=' ')
      factor += 1
```

If the case is different and the condition of the if is ever false, there will be no change in the variable factor. In the case, if the expression factor <= n was true, then it will remain true. An infinite loop can be created effectively to this. The statement that modifies factor must be moved outside of the if statement's body as shown below:

```
while factor <= n:
   if n % factor == 0:
      print(factor, end=' ')
   factor += 1
```

This new version runs correctly as shown:

```
1: 1
2: 1 2
3: 1 3
4: 1 2 4
5: 1 5
6: 1 2 3 6
7: 1 7
8: 1 2 4 8
9: 1 3 9
10: 1 2 5 10
11: 1 11
12: 1 2 3 4 6 12
13: 1 13
14: 1 2 7 14
```

```
15: 1 3 5 15
16: 1 2 4 8 16
17: 1 17
18: 1 2 3 6 9 18
19: 1 19
20: 1 2 4 5 10 20
```

A debugger can be used to step through a program to see why and where an infinite loop arises. Other than this, another common technique is to put print statements in a strategic place in order to examine the values of the variables involved in the loop's control. Augmentation is possible; passing arguments to the original inner loop can be done in this way:

```
while factor <= n:
    print('factor =', factor, ' n =', n)
    if n % factor == 0:
        print(factor, end=' ')
        factor += 1 # <-- Note, still has original error
here
```

The above code has the following output:

```
1: factor = 1 n = 1
1
2: factor = 1 n = 2
1 factor = 2 n = 2
2
3: factor = 1 n = 3
1 factor = 2 n = 3
factor = 2 n = 3
```

```
factor = 2 n = 3
factor = 2 n = 3
factor = 2 n = 3
factor = 2 n = 3
.
.
.
```

While loop enables the program to print continuously the same line until the user interrupts its execution. The output reflects that once factor becomes equal to 2 and n becomes equal to 3 the program's execution becomes trapped in the inner loop. Under the following conditions:

1. 2 < 3 is true, so the loop continues
2. 3 % 2 is equal to 1, so the if statement will not increment factor.

It is imperative that the program increments factor each time via the inner loop. Therefore, the statement incrementing factor must be moved outside of the if's guarded body. By moving it outside, we mean removing it from the if statement's block which means unindenting it.

The code written below is a different version of our factor finder program that uses nested for loops instead of nested while loops. Not only is it slightly shorter, but it also avoids the potential for the misplaced increment of the factor variable. This is due to the reason that the for statement automatically handles the loop variable update.

```
# List the factors of the integers 1...MAX
MAX = 20 # MAX is 20
for n in range(1, MAX + 1): # Consider numbers
1...MAX
        print(end=str(n) + ': ') # Which integer are we
examining?
    for factor in range(1, n + 1): # Try factors 1...n
        if n % factor == 0: # Test to see if factor is a
factor of n
            print(factor, end=' ') # If so, display it
    print() # Move to next line for next n
```

In the final discussion on infinite loops, the preference for using the Debug option under the WingIDE-101 integrated development environment when running our programs. When the program is executed under the Run option, the IDE becomes unresponsive if the program encounters an infinite loop. At that spot, terminating the IDE is the only solution. Under the debugger, a wayward program's execution can easily be interrupted via WingIDE-101's Stop action.

Class

Class is something other than a pattern for a type of object, but it is something more. In Python, a class is not simply a pattern for a type of object, but class is an object itself. Consider the following interactive session:

```
>>> class X:
...        pass   #   An empty class
...
>>> x_obj = X()   #   Make an instance
>>> type(x_obj)
<class '__main__.X'>
>>> type(X)
<class 'type'>
```

It can be seen that the type of a class is type. Every object has a __class__ field that gives the same information as the type function:

```
>>> x_obj.__class__
<class '__main__.X'>
>>> X.__class__
<class 'type'>
```

The name of any class can be obtained via its __name__ field:

```
>>> X.__name__
'X'
>>> x_obj.__class__.__name__
```

```
'X'
>>> X.__class__.__name__
'type'
```

It should be noted that each individual instance of a class maintains its own instance variables. As a class is an instance of type, a class can have its own variables. The term instance variable is reserved for variables within instances of classes; the variables stored in a class object are denoted as class variables. Outside of all methods of a class is a class variable; however, a variable defined within a class. The code written below contains a class variable in order to manage serial numbers of widget objects it manufactures. It is essential that manufactured products have unique serial numbers, and the Widget constructor must ensure the serial number of each widget object is different from any other widget object.

```python
class Widget:
        """ Models a manufactured item. """
        serial_number_source = 0 # Class variable
        def __init__(self):
                """ Make a widget with a unique serial
number. """
                                self.serial_number =
Widget.serial_number_source
                Widget.serial_number_source += 1
        def get_serial_number(self):
                """ Return the widget's serial number. """
                return self.serial_number
if __name__ == '__main__':
```

```
widget_list = []
for i in range(10):
    widget_list.append(Widget())
for w in widget_list:
    print(w.serial_number, end=' ')
print()
```

In the above-written code, the statement serial_number_source = 0 # Class variable appears in class body of Widget but outside the body of any method in the class, which makes serial_number_source a class variable. It is observed that every use of the class variable within a method prefixes the name with the Widget class qualifier.

Class Design: Composition and Inheritance

Class design is the key in object-oriented programming. Developers do not start empty-handed in most of the cases but build new classes from one or more existing classes. The target is for the new class to provide capabilities unavailable in the existing classes. Two key techniques are known for reuse in class design: composition and inheritance.

Composition vs. Inheritance

Both composition and inheritance are effective in many cases. Choice is possible between using composition or inheritance in order to leverage the functionality of an existing class. However, a better choice is not always apparent. The effects of inheritance can be achieved using composition and delegation strictly. A class (CountingStopwatch) uses inheritance to create the CountingStopwatch class from the simpler Stopwatch class. The below-written code defines the class CountingStopwatch2 that behaves identically to CountingStopwatch, but the composition is used in order to reuse the functionality of Stopwatch. Clients will not get any functional differences between a CountingStopwatch instance and a CountingStopwatch2 instance.

```python
from stopwatch import Stopwatch
class CountingStopwatch2:
        """ This counting stopwatch uses composition instead of
            inheritance. """
    def __init__(self):
            # Create a stopwatch object to keep the time
            self.watch = Stopwatch()
            # Set number of starts to zero
            self._count = 0
    def start(self):
            # Count this start message unless the watch already is running
            if not self.watch._running:
                self._count += 1
            # Delegate other work to the stopwatch object
            self.watch.start()
    def stop(self):
            # Delegate to stopwatch object
            self.watch.stop()
    def reset(self):
            # Let the stopwatch object reset the time
```

```
        watch.reset()
            # Reset the count
        self._count = 0
    def elapsed(self):
            # Delegate to stopwatch object
        return self.watch.elapsed()
    def count(self):
        return self._count
```

In order to retrofit countingstopwatch class to use a new counting stopwatch class change the import line:

from countingstopwatch import CountingStopwatch

to be

from countingstopwatch2 import CountingStopwatch2

and change the statement

timer = CountingStopwatch()

to be

timer = CountingStopwatch2()

The program works exactly the same as before only if these changes are made.

With both the composition and inheritance versions, the same goals can be accomplished from the client's perspective, and it does the same. It should be noted that the composition version requires more code. A supposition with inheritance, if a method from the superclass does not need changes, then the programmer omits its definition in the subclass. On the other hand, with composition; however, every method meant to be used by clients in the original class that must have a definition in the new class. A condition is possible here, if the new class does not need to change the method in any way then it simply delegates the work to the contained instance of the original class. It can be seen in the stop and elapsed methods in CountingStopwatch2. It is capable enough to make a big difference in the work required to design a new class if the original class has many methods that do not need any change. The interface of the original class must be maintained to simulate the relationship without using inheritance.

Object-oriented designs, more specifically the good ones, often combine composition and inheritance to achieve useful and important results. A supposition is taken here; we are developing a software system that manages a manufacturing process. A sensor, more specifically a physical temperature sensor attached to a piece of equipment relays temperature information to the software through a software object. The software needs to receive an instance of the TemperatureSensor class from the sensor. The class (TemperatureSensor) provides only two methods which are read and test. Read, which returns the current temperature in degrees Celsius of its attached hardware. In the test method, puts the sensor into a self-test mode. The software on the physical sensor that sends the TemperatureSensor objects to the system is propriety, and its license forbids reverse engineering to change its behavior. You have an issue with the sensors. You are actually stuck with sensors that provide TemperatureSensor objects. Fortunately, as part of the software system that uses the information sent by the sensors is made by the same company that provides the sensors, everything works very well together.

Moreover, one day your company decides for replacement. The decision is taken to replace the existing equipment management software with a new system that is offered by another vendor. The new system has much greater control and monitoring capabilities. The cost of the annual licensing fees is lower than the existing system. However, there is also a problem. However, the new system expects different kinds of sensors on the equipment to monitor. The new software requires sending information via objects of type ThermalValue. The ThermalValue class provides onlyself.watch.stop() def reset(self): # Let the stopwatch object reset the time watch.reset() # Reset the count a temperature method that returns the current temperature in Fahrenheit. The new software does not have the ability to self-test a sensor.

In the overall manufacturing process, hundreds of sensors are used that are very expensive. The cost would be enormous to replace all the perfectly-functioning current sensors with sensors compatible with the new software. Does your company need to upgrade software that can reduce costs and improve the manufacturing process? Does your company want to focus on cost minimization technique?

There are many simple software solutions. The below-written code contains a class that adapts old TemperatureSensor objects to work with the newer software that expects ThermalValue objects:

```
class TemperatureSensorAdapter(ThermalValue):
        """ Adapts a TemperatureSensor object to appear as
        a ThermalValue object. """
    def __init__(self, sensor):
        """ sensor is the TemperatureSensor object to adapt """
        self._sensor = sensor
    def temperature(self):
        """ Converts the sensor input from Celsius to Fahrenheit """
        return 9 * self._sensor.read() / 5 + 32
```

Intercepting the TemperatureSensor object from an existing sensor is to be done. Also, create a new TemperatureSensorAdapter object from that TemperatureSensor object. Now, send the TemperatureSensorAdapter object on to a new management and monitoring software. The new system receives a ThermalValue object; it is due to the reason that a TemperatureSensorAdapter object is a ThermalValue object. Inheritance guarantees a relationship. The temperature method communicates most of its work to the contained TemperatureSensor object. The TemperatureSensor object gives the temperature. A conversion should take place. The method merely needs to convert the temperature from Celsius to Fahrenheit to conform to the expectations of the new system.

It is known that ThermalValue objects have no test method; it is further known that the new software system will never attempt to call it. The TemperatureSensor provides functionalities that will never be used so that it can be ignored safely.

It should be noted that this solution uses both inheritance and composition. It is actually an example of an object-oriented design pattern. A design pattern actually provides a solution to a commonly occurring problem in software design. A design pattern has no exact solution for a given problem. Design pattern instead shows how techniques (inheritance and composition) may be applied to solve problems of a particular kind.

It should further be highlighted that each design pattern has its own name. The design pattern involved in our TemperatureSensorAdapter class is aptly named adapter. The TemperatureSensorAdapter class adapts both the interface and computation. The adapter pattern is sometimes called the wrapper pattern. The reason is that the object serves as a wrapper around another object. In our case, a TemperatureSensorAdapter object wraps a ThermalValue object.

For class reuse, which should you use when it comes to choosing composition or inheritance? It is wisely said that composition is preferred over inheritance. The reasons for preferring composition over inheritance are many. The composition is more flexible than inheritance when it comes to the cost of potentially more code to write. When it is tempted to use inheritance, ask yourself if an instance, the new class philosophically is an instance of the original class. If this relationship makes sense, then inheritance is the better choice; otherwise, the composition should be used.

Let's take a scenario. A motor vehicle is considered for this scenario. The drive train of a motor vehicle contains sounds like composition known as axles and wheels, among other containing parts. It is now said that each axle assembly consists of an axle and two wheels. Does it make any sense in order to derive an axle assembly class from an axle class and add a left wheel object and a right wheel object as new instance variables? Is an axle assembly an axle? Definitely not, an axle assembly consists of an axle and two wheels (has a relationship). So, the composition is the better choice in this case.

Multi-way Decision Statements

A simple if/else statement can select from between two execution paths. We know how to select from among three options. What if exactly one of many actions should be taken?

The nested if/else statements are needed, and the form of these nested if/else statements are shown in the below code.

```python
value = int(input("Please enter an integer in the range 0...5: "))
if value < 0:
    print("Too small")
else:
    if value == 0:
        print("zero")
    else:
        if value == 1:
            print("one")
        else:
            if value == 2:
                print("two")
            else:
        if value == 3:
            print("three")
        else:
```

```
        if value == 4:
            print("four")
                else:
                    if value == 5:
                    print("five")
                else:
                            print("Too large")
print("Done")
```

We can observe the above code as:

- It prints exactly one of eight messages, but it also depends upon the user's input.

- It should be noted that if the block contains a single printing statement and each else block, except for the last one, contains an if statement. Furthermore, the control logic forces the program execution to check each condition in turn. Which condition goes right, and which one goes wrong? In any scenario of conditions like this, the first condition that matches wins, and its corresponding if the body will be executed. In the case, if none of the conditions are true, then the program prints the last else condition, 'Too large' in the above case.

As a consequence of the required formatting of the above code, the mass of text drifts

to the right as more conditions are checked. Python provides support of the multi-way conditional construct known as if/elif/else that permits a more manageable textual structure for programs that needs to check or execute many conditions.

The code below uses the if/elif/else statement to avoid the rightward code drift.

Listing 4.18: restyleddigittoword.py

```python
value = int(input("Please enter an integer in the range 0...5: "))
if value < 0:
    print("Too small")
elif value == 0:
    print("zero")
elif value == 1:
    print("one")
elif value == 2:
    print("two")
elif value == 3:
    print("three")
elif value == 4:
    print("four")
elif value == 5:
    print("five")
else:
```

```
    print("Too large")
print("Done")
```

The term elif is used as a contraction of else and if; if you read elif as else if, you can see how we can transform the code fragment

```
else:
    if value == 2:
        print("two")
```

Code like this changes into

```
elif value == 2:
print("two")
```

In the above case.

The conditional if/elif/else statement is valuable for selecting exactly one block of code to check or execute from several options. The if part of a conditional if/elif/else statement is mandatory while the else part is optional.

After the if part and before else part (if present), many elif blocks can be used if necessary.

The general form of an if/elif/else statement is shown below:

```
if  condition-1  :
        block-1

elif condition-2 :
        block-2

elif condition-3 :
        block-3

elif condition-4 :
        block-4
            •
            •
            •
else:
        default-block
```

The code below uses a conditional if/elif/else statement to transform a numeric date in month/

day format to an expanded US English form and an international Spanish form; for example, 2/14 would be converted to 'February 14' (US English) and '14 febrero' (Spanish).

Listing 4.19: datetransformer.py

```
month = int(input("Please enter the month as a
number (1-12): "))
day = int(input("Please enter the day of the month: "))
# Translate month into English
if month == 1:
    print("January ", end='')
elif month == 2:
    print("February ", end='')
elif month == 3:
    print("March ", end='')
```

```python
elif month == 4:
    print("April ", end=")
elif month == 5:
    print("May ", end=")
elif month == 6:
    print("June ", end=")
elif month == 7:
    print("July ", end=")
elif month == 8:
    print("August ", end=")
elif month == 9:
    print("September ", end=")
elif month == 10:
    print("October ", end=")
elif month == 11:
    print("November ", end=")
else:
print("December ", end=")
# Add the day
print(day, 'or', day, end=")
# Translate month into Spanish
if month == 1:
    print(" de enero")
elif month == 2:
    print(" de febrero")
elif month == 3:
    print(" de marzo")
elif month == 4:
    print(" de abril")
```

```
elif month == 5:
    print(" de mayo")
elif month == 6:
    print(" de junio")
elif month == 7:
    print(" de julio")
elif month == 8:
    print(" de agosto")
elif month == 9:
    print(" de septiembre")
elif month == 10:
    print(" de octubre")
elif month == 11:
    print(" de noviembre")
else:
print(" de diciembre")
```

A simple execution of the above code shows

```
Please enter the month as a number (1-12): 5
Please enter the day of the month: 20
May 20 or 20 de mayo
```

The multi-conditional if/elif/else statements that include the optional else will execute exactly one of its blocks. The first condition that evaluates to true selects the block to execute. An if/elif/else statement that omits the else block may fail to execute the code any line of its blocks if none of its conditions is True.

Logic Complexity

There are many difficult and complication conditional statements, but Python provides the tools to construct those complicated conditional statements. It is important to resist the urge to make things overly complex. Composing Boolean expressions with and, or, and not allows us to build conditions with arbitrarily complex logic which will be tested in many ways. There are many ways to achieve the same effect; suppose, the following four Boolean expressions are equivalent:

```
not (a == b and c != d)
not (a == b and not (c == d))
not (a == b) or not (c != d)
a != b or c == d
```

The four expressions are logically equivalent; they create various degrees of complication.

Some situations require some more complicated logic to achieve the desired program behavior, but generally, the simplest and easy logic that works is better than more complex equivalent logic for several reasons:

- It is easier to understand simpler logic
- It is easy to write and get work of simpler logic. In more complicated expressions, the risk of typographical errors increases that can manifest themselves as logic errors. These

errors are difficult to find and correct in code complexities.

- Simpler logic can be more efficient. Every relational comparison and Boolean operation executed by a running program must require machine cycles. The expression not (a == b and not (c == d)) performs more operations of up to five separate operations: == twice, not twice, and once. If 'a' does not equal 'b', then the expression performs only two operations (== and the outer not) it results due to the short-circuit Boolean evaluation of the and. Compare this expression to the following equivalent expression: a != b or c == d. This expression can be evaluated faster by an executing program, as it involves at most three operations: !=, ==, and or. If 'a' is not equal to 'b', then the execution short-circuits or happens to evaluates only the != operation.
- It is easier to modify and extend the simpler logic.

Let's consider the task of computing the maximum value of four integers entered by the user as user input. Below is the code:

Listing 4.28: max4a.py

```
# Get input values from user
```

```
print("Please enter four integer values.")
num1 = int(input("Enter number 1: "))
num2 = int(input("Enter number 2: "))
num3 = int(input("Enter number 3: "))
num4 = int(input("Enter number 4: "))
# Compute the maximum value
if num1 >= num2 and num1 >= num3 and num1 >= num4:
max = num1
elif num2 >= num1 and num2 >= num3 and num2 >= num4:
max = num2
elif num3 >= num1 and num3 >= num2 and num3 >= num4:
max = num3
else: # The maximum must be num4 at this point
max = num4
# Report result
print("The maximum number entered was:", max)
```

The above code uses a multi-way if/elif/else construction in order to select the correct value to assign to its maximum variable.

The above code works correctly for any four integers a user may enter, but its logic is a little complicated. A different strategy will be considered for our selection logic. All variables have a meaning, and their names should reflect their meaning in some way. The maximum variable means "maximum I have determined so far." The following is the outline of our new approach to the solution:

1. The Set max is equal to n1. It is known at the moment, n1 is the biggest number because max and n1 have the same value.
2. Then compare max to n2. Condition creation, If n2 is larger than max, change max to have n2's value to reflect the fact that n2 is determined larger; if n2 is not larger than max, we have no reason to change max, so there is no need to change it.
3. Then compare max to n3. Condition creation, if n3 is larger than max, change max to have n3's value to reflect the fact that n3 is determined larger; if n3 is not larger than max, we have no reason to change max, so there is no need to change it.
4. Then compare max to n4. Condition creation, if n4 is larger than max, change max to have n4's value to reflect the fact that n4 is determined larger; if n4 is not larger than max, we have no reason to change max, so there is no need to change it.

In the end, the meaning of the max variable remains the same—"maximum I have determined so far." However, after comparing the max to all the input variables, it is known to be the maximum value of all the four input numbers. The extra variable max is not strictly necessary but makes thinking about the problem and its solution easier.

The code below uses the revised selection logic to provide an alternative to the above code.

Listing 4.29: max4b.py

```
# Get input values from user
print("Please enter four integer values.")
num1 = int(input("Enter number 1: "))
num2 = int(input("Enter number 2: "))
num3 = int(input("Enter number 3: "))
num4 = int(input("Enter number 4: "))
# Compute the maximum value
max = num1
if num2 > max:
    max = num2
if num3 > max:
    max = num3
if num4 > max:
    max = num4
# Report result
print("The maximum number entered was:", max)
```

This code uses very simple and sequential if statements to assign the correct value to its max variable eventually.

This code always performs three > comparisons and at most four assignments without considering the values provided by the user. The source code we discussed before contains many more Boolean operations than this code, but due to short-circuit evaluation, the code with Boolean operations actually can outperform this code in some situations. The simpler logic is actually there is no guarantee of better performance. Both the programs are super simple. However, no difference in execution speed will be perceived by users.

What changes are needed to make to both the codes (The one with Booleans and the simple one with if statement)?

Adding this capability to the Boolean code that actually forces us to modify each and every condition in the program, adding a check against a new num5 variable.

An additional elif check must be provided since we will need to select from among five possible assignments to the max variable. In the simple code (the one with if statement) however, an extra sequential if statement needs addition in order to check a new simple condition.

In loops introduction, loops have the ability to execute statements repeatedly. Learners can easily adapt the sequential if the approach to allow users to type in as many numbers as they like and then have the program report the maximum number the user entered maybe as user input. The multi-way conditions if/elif/else approach with the more logic complexities which cannot be adapted in this manner. Not only is the sequential if version cleaner and simpler; its capabilities can be extended more.

Functions and Modules

Functions are used in complex cases to get rid of lengthy codes. There are many functions used by programmers which will be discussed. Furthermore, a Python module is simply a file that contains Python code. The name of the file dictates the name of the module; for example, a file named math.py contains the functions available from the standard math module.

The modules are important, having the standard modules that contain functions that can be used in many different programs. The Python standard library contains thousands of functions distributed throughout more than 230 modules. These modules can cover a wide range of application domains. One of the modules is known as the built-ins module. The built-in module contains all the functions including print, input, etc. These built-in functions make up only a very small fraction of all the functions the standard library provides. Programmers must use one or more import statements within a program or within the interactive interpreter to gain access to the remaining standard functions.

from *module* import *function list*

It is the general form of a statement that imports a subset of a module available function.

These standard modules are stored somewhere on the computer's hard drive by the Python distribution for a given platform. It is the interpreter who knows where to locate these standard modules when an executing program needs to import them. It is not uncommon for a complex program to import a dozen separate modules to get all functions it needs to do its function.

Python has a number of ways to import functions from a module. We will see an emphasis and concentration on the two most commonly used techniques.

Importing the sqrt function;

The imported square root function is as follows:

from math import sqrt

A program that needs to compute square roots, common logarithms, and the trigonometric cosine function could use different import statements: For example, from math import sqrt, log10, cos.

This statement enables only the sqrt, log10, and cos functions from the math module available to the program. The math module offers many other mathematical functions including the 'atan' function that computes the arctangent but this limited import statement does not provide these other definitions to the interpreter. The image here shows the general form of this kind of import statement. Such an import statement is an appropriate statement for smaller Python programs that use a small number of functions from a module.

This kind of import statement enables callers to use an imported function's simple name, as in
y = sqrt(x)

If the case is different, and a program requires many different functions from a module, listing them all individually can become unwieldy. Python provides a way to import everything a module has to offer. It can be seen in further discussions.

Rather than importing one or more components of a module, the entire module can be imported, as shown right here.
import math

The image below shows the general form of this kind of import statement. This import statement makes all of the functions of the module as well-available functions to the program, but in order to use a function, the caller must attach or mention the module's name during the call. The code below demonstrates the call notation:

y = math.sqrt(x)
print(math.log10(100))

It should be noted that the math.prefix attached to the calls of the sqrt and log10 functions. We call a composite name (module-name.function-name), a qualified name like this. The qualified name includes the module name and function name.

import *module list*

      It is the general form statement that imports an entire module.

Many programmers prefer to have this approach due to the complete name unambiguously identifies the function with its module. A large complex program could import the math module and a different third-party module called extramath. Consider the extramath module provide its own sqrt function. There can be no mistaking to the fact that the sqrt being called in the expression math.sqrt(16), is the one provided by the math module. It is impossible for a program to use their simple names simultaneously within a program and import the sqrt functions separately from both modules. Does y = sqrt(x) intend to use math's sqrt or extramath's sqrt?

It should be noted that a statement such as from math import sqrt does not import the entire module. Code under this import statement may use only the simple name, sqrt, and cannot use the qualified name, math.sqrt.

As programs get larger and more complex until the end, the import entire module approach becomes more compelling.

The qualified function names improve the code readability and avoid name clashes between modules that provide functions with identical names.

Qualified names ensure that names we create ourselves will not clash with any names that modules may provide. Own functions can also be written depending on what the program requires.

The Built-in Functions

Functions also include print, input, int, float, str, and type, called built-in functions. These functions and many others reside in a module named _ _built-ins_ _. The __built-ins__ module is special due to its components are automatically available to any Python program with—no import statement is required. The full name of the print function is _built-ins_.print, although chances are you will rarely see its full name written in a Python program. Its fully qualified name can be verified in the interpreter:

```
>>> print('Hi')
Hi
>>> __builtins__.print('Hi')
Hi
>>> print
```

```
<built-in function print>
>>> __builtins__.print
<built-in function print>
>>> id(print)
9506056
>>> id(__builtins__.print)
9506056
```

The above interactive sequence verifies that the names print and _builtins_.print refers to the same function object. The 'id' function is another __builtins__ function. The expression id(x) evaluates to the actual address in memory of an object named 'x.' Since id(print) and id(__builtins__.print) evaluate to the same value, it is known that both the names correspond to the same function object.

The 'dir' function, which stands for directory, reveals all the components that a module has to offer.

The below interactive sequence prints the __builtins__ components:

```
>>> dir(__builtins__)
['ArithmeticError', 'AssertionError', 'AttributeError',
'BaseException',
'BlockingIOError', 'BrokenPipeError', 'BufferError',
'Bytes Warning',
'ChildProcessError', 'ConnectionAbortedError',
'ConnectionError',
```

'ConnectionRefusedError', 'ConnectionResetError',
'Depre cationWarning',

'EOFError', 'Ellipsis', 'EnvironmentError', 'Exception',
'False',

'FileExistsError', 'FileNotFoundError', 'FloatingP
ointError',

'FutureWarning', 'GeneratorExit', 'IOError',
'ImportError',

'ImportWarning', 'IndentationError', 'IndexError',
'Interrup tedError',

'IsADirectoryError', 'KeyError', 'KeyboardInterrupt',
'LookupError',

'MemoryError', 'NameError', 'None', 'NotADirectoryEr
ror',

'NotImplemented', 'NotImplementedError', 'OSError',
'OverflowError',

'PendingDeprecationWarning', 'PermissionError',
'ProcessL ookupError',

'ReferenceError', 'ResourceWarning', 'RuntimeError',
'RuntimeWarning',

'StopIteration', 'SyntaxError', 'SyntaxWarning',
'SystemError',

'SystemExit', 'TabError', 'TimeoutError', 'True',
'TypeError',

'UnboundLocalError', 'UnicodeDecodeError',
'UnicodeEn codeError',

'UnicodeError', 'UnicodeTranslateError',
'UnicodeWarning', 'UserWarning',

'ValueError', 'Warning', 'WindowsError', 'Zero
DivisionError',

```
'__build_class__', '__debug__', '__doc__',
'__import__', '__loader__',
'__name__', '__package__', '__spec__', 'abs', 'all',
'any', 'ascii',
'bin', 'bool', 'bytearray', 'bytes', 'callable', 'chr',
'classmethod',
'compile', 'complex', 'copyright', 'credits', 'delattr',
'dict', 'dir',
'divmod', 'enumerate', 'eval', 'exec', 'exit', 'filter', 'float',
'format', 'frozenset', 'getattr ', 'globals', 'hasattr',
'hash', 'help',
'hex', 'id', 'input', 'int', 'isinstance', 'issubclass', 'iter',
'len',
'license', 'list', 'locals', 'map', 'max', 'memoryview',
'min', 'next',
'object', 'oct', 'open', 'ord', 'pow', 'print', 'property',
'quit',
'range', 'repr', 'reversed', 'round', 'set', 'setattr', 'slice',
'sorted', 'staticmethod', 'str', 'sum', 'super', 'tuple',
'type',
'vars', 'zip']
>>>
```

A module contains other things besides functions, but it is not always the case. Most of the names in the first 18 lines or so of the_ _built-ins_ _ module directory listings are types defined by the module. Most of the names in the last 11 lines are functions. The table list contains many recognizable names: dir, bool, float, id, input, int, print, round, range, str, and type functions.

The _ _built-ins_ _ module provides a common core of general functions that are useful to any Python program without considering its application area. Python provides other standard modules, are aimed at specific application domains, such as mathematics, system administration, text processing, file processing, graphics, and Internet protocols, and multimedia. Programs that require more domain-specific functionality must import the appropriate modules that provide the needed services.

The _ _built-ins_ _ module also includes a help function. In the interactive interpreter, the help function can be used to print human-readable information on specific functions in the current namespace. The following sequence shows how the 'help' works:

```
>>> help(print)
Help on built-in function print in module builtins:
print(...)
        print(value, ..., sep=' ', end='\n', file=sys.stdout,
flush=False)
        Prints the values to a stream, or to sys.stdout by
default.
    Optional keyword arguments:
        file: a file-like object (stream); defaults to the
current sys.stdout.
        sep: string inserted between values, default a
space.
```

    end: string appended after the last value, default a
newline.
    flush: whether to forcibly flush the stream.

>>> help(input)
Help on built-in function input in module builtins:
input(...)
    input([prompt]) -> string

        Read a string from standard input. The trailing
newline is stripped.
        If the user hits EOF (Unix: Ctl-D, Windows: Ctl-
Z+Return), raise EOFError.
        On Unix, GNU readline is used if enabled. The
prompt string, if given,
    is printed without a trailing newline before reading.

>>> help(sqrt)
Traceback (most recent call last):
    File "<stdin>", line 1, in <module>
NameError: name 'sqrt' is not defined
>>> help(math.sqrt)
Traceback (most recent call last):
    File "<stdin>", line 1, in <module>
NameError: name 'math' is not defined
>>> import math
>>> help(math.sqrt)
Help on built-in function sqrt in module math:
sqrt(...)
    sqrt(x)
    Return the square root of x.

It should be noted that 'help' was powerless to provide information about 'math.sqrt' function until we imported the math module.

Standard Mathematical Functions

The standard mathematical functions enable a programmer for fast computation and problem-solving. The standard math module provides much of the functionality of a scientific calculator. The following table lists only a few of the available functions.

Table: A few of the functions from the math module:

math Module
sqrt Computes the square root of a number: sqrt(x) = $\sqrt{x}$

| exp
Computes e raised a power: exp(x) = e^x |

| log
Computes the natural logarithm of a number: log(x) = $\log_e x = \ln x$ |

| log10 |

Computes the common logarithm of a number: $\log(x)$ = log10 x

cos

This function computes the cosine of a value specified in radians: $\cos(x)$ = cosx; other trigonometric functions include sine, tangent, arc cosine, arc sine, arc tangent, hyperbolic cosine, hyperbolic sine, and hyperbolic tangent

pow

Raises one number to a power of another: $pow(x, y)$ = x^y

degrees

Converts a value in radians to degrees: $degrees(x)$ = $(\Pi/180)x$

radians

Converts a value in degrees to radians: $radians(x)$ = $(180/\Pi)x$

fabs

Computes the absolute value of a number: $fabs(x)$ = $|x|$

The math module also defines the values pi (p) and e (e). The following interactive sequence reveals the math module's full directory of components:

```
>>> import math
>>> dir(math)
['__doc__', '__loader__', '__name__', '__package__',
'__spec__', 'acos',
'acosh', 'asin', 'asinh', 'atan', 'atan2', 'atanh', 'ceil',
'copysign',
'cos', 'cosh', 'degrees', 'e', 'erf', 'erfc', 'exp', 'expm1',
'fabs',
'factorial', 'floor', 'fmod', 'frexp', 'fsum', 'g amma',
'hypot',
'isfinite', 'isinf', 'isnan', 'ldexp', 'lgamma', 'log', 'log10',
'log1p',
'log2', 'modf', 'pi', 'pow', 'radians', 'sin', 'sinh', 'sqrt',
'tan',
'tanh', 'trunc']
>>>
```

Most of the names in the directory represent functions.

The actual parameter is said to be the parameter passed by the caller. The parameter specified by the function is called the formal parameter. During a function, call the first actual parameter is assigned to the first formal parameter, the second actual parameter is assigned to the second formal parameter. The caller must take care to put the arguments they pass in the proper order when calling a function. For example, the call math.pow (10, 2) computes 102 = 100, but the call math.pow (2, 10) computes 210 = 1,024.

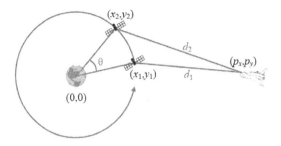

It is the problem of orbital distance. In the diagram, the satellite begins at point (x1, y1), a distance of d1 from the spacecraft. A satellite orbit takes it to the point (x2, y2) after an angle of 0 rotations; the distance to its new location is d2.

The math module must be imported by any Python program that uses any of these mathematical functions.

The functions in the math module are ideal for solving problems like the one shown in the above image.

A supposition has taken place. A spacecraft has a fixed location in space at some distance from a planet. A satellite has an influence on the planet and is orbiting the planet in a circular orbit. Computation is needed of how much farther away the satellite will be from the spacecraft when it has progressed 0 degrees along its orbital path.

The origin of our coordinate system (0, 0) is located at the center of the planet. The origin location also corresponds to the center of the circular orbital path of the satellite. The satellite is located at some point (x, y) and the spacecraft is stationary at point (px, py). The spacecraft is located in the same plane as the orbiting satellite. Computation is needed of the distances between the moving point (satellite) and the fixed point (spacecraft), as the satellite orbits the planet.

Facts from mathematics provide solutions to the following two problems:

1. Problem: We must recompute the location of the moving point as it moves along the circle.

Solution: Given an initial position (x;y) of a point, a rotation of q degrees around the origin will yield a new point at (x', y'), where:

$x' = x \cos q - y \sin q$
$y' = x \sin q + y \cos q$

2. Problem: The distance between the moving point and the fixed point as the moving point moves to a new position, must be recalculated.

Solution: The distance d in the above image between the two points (px, py) and (x, y) is given by the formula

$$d = \frac{\sqrt{(x - Px)^2 - (y - Py)^2}}{1}$$

The following code uses the above mathematical results to compute a table of distances that span a complete orbit of the satellite:

```python
# Use some functions and values from the math module
from math import sqrt, sin, cos, pi, radians
# Get coordinates of the stationary spacecraft, (px, py)
px = float(input("Enter x coordinate of spacecraft: "))
py = float(input("Enter y coordinate of spacecraft: "))
# Get starting coordinates of satellite, (x1, y1)
x = float(input("Enter initial satellite x coordinate: "))
y = float(input("Enter initial satellite y coordinate: "))
# Convert 60 degrees to radians to be able to use the trigonometric functions
rads = radians(60)
# Precompute the cosine and sine of the angle
COS_theta = cos(rads)
SIN_theta = sin(rads)
# Make a complete revolution (6*60 = 360 degrees)
for increment in range(0, 7):
    # Compute the distance to the satellite
    dist = sqrt((px - x)*(px - x) + (py - y)*(py - y))
```

```
            print('Distance  to  satellite  {0:10.2f}
km'.format(dist))
    # Compute the satellite's new (x, y) location after
rotating by 60 degrees
```

x, y = x*COS_theta - y*SIN_theta, x*SIN_theta +
y*COS_theta

The code above prints the distances from the
spacecraft to the satellite in 60-degree orbit
increments.

A sample run of the above code prints:

```
Enter x coordinate of spacecraft: 100000
Enter y coordinate of spacecraft: 0
Enter initial satellite x coordinate: 20000
Enter initial satellite y coordinate: 0
Distance to satellite 80000.00 km
Distance to satellite 91651.51 km
Distance to satellite 111355.29 km
Distance to satellite 120000.00 km
Distance to satellite 111355.29 km
Distance to satellite 91651.51 km
```

The user enters the point (100,000,0), firstly, and
then the tuple (20,000,0). Observing the satellite
begins 80,000 km away from the spacecraft, and the
distance increases to the maximum are 120,000 km
when it is at the far side of its orbit. The satellite

returns to its starting place ready for the next orbit, eventually.

The code above uses tuple assignment to update the 'x' and 'y' variables:

```
# Uses tuple assignment
x, y = x*COS_theta - y*SIN_theta, x*SIN_theta + y*COS_theta
```

If instead of using two separate assignment statements, care should be taken for—the following code does not work the same way:

```
# Does not work correctly
x = x*COS_theta - y*SIN_theta
y = x*SIN_theta + y*COS_theta
```

This is due to the value of 'x' which is used in the second assignment statement is the new value of 'x' computed by the first assignment statement. The original x value is used by the tuple assignment version in both the computations.

If it is needed to use two assignment statements rather than a single tuple assignment, an extra variable should be introduced for not to lose the original value of 'x':

```
new_x = x*COS_theta - y*SIN_theta # Compute new x value
```

```
y = x*SIN_theta + y*COS_theta # Compute new y
value using original x
x = new_x # Update x
```

The square root function can be used to improve the efficiency of the code listing primes. Instead of trying all the potential factors of 'n' up to n-1, only try potential factors up to pn are needed. The code below uses the sqrt function to reduce the number of potential factors the program needs to consider.

```
from math import sqrt
max_value = int(input('Display primes up to what
value? '))
value = 2 # Smallest prime number

while value <= max_value:
    # See if value is prime
    is_prime = True # Provisionally, value is prime
    # Try all possible factors from 2 to value - 1
    trial_factor = 2
    root = sqrt(value) # Compute the square root of
value

    while trial_factor <= root:
        if value % trial_factor == 0:
            is_prime = False # Found a factor
            break # No need to continue; it is NOT
prime

            trial_factor += 1 # Try the next potential
factor
```

```
    if is_prime:
            print(value, end= ' ') # Display the prime
number
            value += 1 # Try the next potential prime
number
print() # Move cursor down to next line
```

Time Functions

Another type of functions is called time functions. The time module contains a number of functions relating to time. Two will be considered: clock and sleep.

The time.clock function enables the measurement of time parts of a program's execution. The time.clock function returns a floating-point value that represents elapsed time in seconds. What the time.clock function does on other systems. On Unix-like systems (Linux and Mac OS X), time.clock returns the numbers of seconds elapsed since the program began to execute.

Under the Microsoft Windows, time.clock returns the number of seconds since the first call to time.clock. In either case, with two calls to the time.clock function elapsed time can be measured. The code below measures how long it takes a user to enter a character from the keyboard.

```
from time import clock
print("Enter your name: ", end="")
start_time = clock()
name = input()
elapsed = clock() - start_time
```

```
print(name, "it took you", elapsed, "seconds to respond")
```

The following represents the interaction of program with a particularly slow typist:

```
Enter your name: Rick
Rick it took you 7.246477029927183 seconds to respond
```

The code below measures the time it takes for a Python program to add up all the integers
from 1 to 100,000,000.

```
from time import clock
sum = 0 # Initialize sum accumulator
start = clock() # Start the stopwatch
for n in range(1, 100000001): # Sum the numbers
    sum += n
elapsed = clock() - start # Stop the stopwatch
print("sum:", sum, "time:", elapsed) # Report results
```

On one system the above code reports:

```
sum:   5000000050000000   time:
24.922694830903826
```

The list below measures how long it takes a program
to count all the prime numbers

up to 10,000

```python
from time import clock
max_value = 10000
count = 0
start_time = clock() # Start timer
# Try values from 2 (smallest prime number) to
max_value
for value in range(2, max_value + 1):
    # See if value is prime
    is_prime = True # Provisionally, value is prime
    # Try all possible factors from 2 to value - 1
    for trial_factor in range(2, value):
        if value % trial_factor == 0:
            is_prime = False # Found a factor
            break # No need to continue; it is NOT
prime
    if is_prime:
        count += 1 # Count the prime number
print() # Move cursor down to next line
elapsed = clock() - start_time # Stop the timer
print("Count:", count, " Elapsed time:", elapsed,
"sec")
```

On one system, the program produces:

```
Count: 1229    Elapsed time: 1.6250698114336175
sec
```

The repeated runs a report on an execution time of approximately 1.6 seconds to count all the prime numbers up to 10,000, consistently.

Exact times will vary and usually depend on the speed of the computer.

```
from math import sqrt
from time import clock
max_value = 10000
count = 0
value = 2 # Smallest prime number
start = clock() # Start the stopwatch
while value <= max_value:
    # See if value is prime
    is_prime = True # Provisionally, value is prime
    # Try all possible factors from 2 to value - 1
    trial_factor = 2
    root = sqrt(value)
    while trial_factor <= root:
        if value % trial_factor == 0:
            is_prime = False # Found a factor
            break # No need to continue; it is NOT prime
        trial_factor += 1 # Try the next potential factor
    if is_prime:
        count += 1 # Count the prime number
```

```
        value += 1 # Try the next potential prime
number
elapsed = clock() - start # Stop the stopwatch
print("Count:", count, " Elapsed time:", elapsed,
"sec")
```

What does the time.sleep function do? It actually
suspends the program's execution for a specified
number of seconds. The code below counts down
from 10 with one second intervals between numbers.

```
from time import sleep
for count in range(10, -1, -1): # Range 10, 9, 8, ..., 0
    print(count) # Display the count
    sleep(1) # Suspend execution for 1 second
```

For controlling the speed of graphical animations, the
time.sleep function is used.

System-specific Functions

The 'sys module' provides numerous functions and
variables that give programmers access to system-
specific information. One useful function is 'exit' that
terminates an executing program. The code below
uses the sys.exit function to end the execution of the
program after it prints ten numbers.

```
import sys
sum = 0
while True:
```

```
x = int(input('Enter a number (999 ends):'))
if x == 999:
    sys.exit(0)
sum += x
print('Sum is', sum)
```

What the sys.exit function does in the above code? The sys.exit function actually accepts a single integer argument, which is passed back to the operating system when the program completes. The value zero reflects the successful completion of the program; a non-zero value represents the program terminating due to a kind of error.

Python List

A list is actually a kind of container or an object that holds a collection of other objects. It represents a sequence of data. The list is similar to a string, but a string can hold only characters while a list has the ability to hold any Python object. A list needs not to be homogeneous, which means that the elements of a list do not all have to be of the same type. Like any other variable, a list variable can be local or global, and it must be defined before its use. The following code fragment defines a list named as 'lst' that holds the integer values 2, -3, 0, 4, -1:

lst = [2, -3, 0, 4, -1]

It should be noted that the right-hand side of the assignment statement is a literal list. The elements of the list appear within the square brackets ([ ]), and commas are used to separate elements from one another.

The following statement assigns the empty list to a variable named 'a':

a = [ ]

The list literals and lists referenced can be printed through variables:

```
lst = [2, -3, 0, 4, -1] # Assign the list
```

```
print([2, -3, 0, 4, -1]) # Print a literal list
print(lst) # Print a list via a variable
```

The code prints:

```
[2, -3, 0, 4, -1]
```

The elements in a list can be accessed via their position or place within the list. We access individual elements of a list using square brackets:

```
lst = [2, -3, 0, 4, -1] # Assign the list
lst[0] = 5 # Make the first element 5
print(lst[1]) # Print the second element
lst[4] = 12 # Make the last element 12
print(lst) # Print a list variable
print([10, 20, 30][1]) # Print second element of literal
list
```

This code prints:

```
-3
[5, -3, 0, 4, 12]
20
```

The number within the square brackets is called the index. A non-negative index reflects the distance from the beginning of the list. The expression lst[0] reflects the element at the very beginning (a distance of zero from the beginning) of 'lst,' and 'lst[1]' is the second element (a distance of one away from the beginning). The expression 'a[3]' can be read as "a sub-three," where the index 3 represents a subscript. The subscript terminology is borrowed from mathematicians. The mathematicians use subscripts to reference elements in a mathematical vector or matrix. For example, V2 represents the second element in vector V.

Unlike the convention often used in mathematics, however, the first element in a list is at position 'zero' and not at position 'one.' The index indicates the distance from the beginning. Thus, the very first element is at a distance of zero from the beginning of the list. The first element of the list 'a' is a[0]. As a consequence of a zero-beginning index, if list 'a' holds 'n' elements, the last element in 'a' is a[n-1], and it is not a[n].

Below figure contains three elements. Each number below the list represents the index of each element.

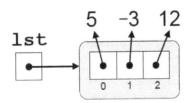

Consider a list 'a' with elements 'n,' and i is an integer such that 0 is less or equal to 'i,' and 'i' is less than 'n,' then a[n] is an element in the list.

The place of elements can also be represented by negative index numbers. A negative list index represents a negative offset from an imaginary element one past the end of the list.

For the list a, a[-1] represents the last element in a. The expression a[-2] represents the second-last element, and so forth. If 'a' contains 'n' elements, the expression a[0] corresponds to lst[-n].

Listing following code reflects the use of negative indices to print a list in the reverse direction.

```
def main( ):
data = [10, 20, 30, 40, 50, 60]
# Print the individual elements with negative indices
print(data[-1])
print(data[-2])
print(data[-3])
print(data[-4])
print(data[-5])
print(data[-6])
main( ) # Execute main
```

Listing prints:

```
60
50
40
30
20
10
```

The above figure visualizes the list assigned as:

lst = [5, -3, 12]

The following list demonstrates that lists may be heterogeneous. It means that a list can hold elements of varying types:

```
collection = [24.2, 4, 'word', print, 19, -0.03, 'end']
print(collection[0])
print(collection[1])
print(collection[2])
print(collection[3])
print(collection[4])
print(collection[5])
print(collection[6])
print(collection)
```

The following are the Listing prints:

```
24.2
```

```
4
word
<built-in function print>
19
-0.03
end
[24.2, 4, 'word', <built-in function print>, 19, -0.03,
'end']
```

It can be seen that a single list can hold integers,
float numbers, strings, and even functions. A list can
also hold other lists inside it; the following code:

```
col = [23, [9.3, 11.2, 99.0], [23], [ ], 4, [0, 0]]
print(col)
```

Prints:

```
[23, [9.3, 11.2, 99.0], [23], [ ], 4, [0, 0]]
```

Four of the elements of the list col are themselves
lists.

List Traversal

List traversal is very important in many application
developments. List traversal is actually the action of
moving through a list visiting each element is known
as traversal. A list is a kind of object which can be

iterated. A for loop can be used to visit each element in order within a list.

The following list uses a for loop:

```
collection = [24.2, 4, 'word', print, 19, -0.03, 'end']
for item in collection:
    print(item) # Print each element
                #The built-in function len returns the
number of elements in a list: The code segment
print(len([2, 4, 6, 8]))
a = [10, 20, 30]
print(len(a))
```

Prints:

```
4
3
```

The term 'len' stands for length. The index of the last element in the list 'lst' is lst[len(lst) - 1].

It can be noticed in other programming languages, you may be tempted to use len and an explicit list index with a for a loop as shown in the below figure instead of the code in the above figure.

```
collection = [24.2, 4, 'word', print, 19, -0.03, 'end']
for i in range(len(collection)): # Not the preferred way
to traverse a list
    print(collection[i]) # Print each element
```

How to print elements in a list in the reverse order? The familiar code for i in range can be used to do so. Construct and use an explicit index to count backwards:

```
nums = [2, 4, 6, 8]
# Print last element to first (zero index) element
for i in range(len(nums) - 1, -1, -1):
    print(nums[i])
```

It prints:

```
8
6
4
2
```

An even better way to iterate over list elements from back to front is to use Python's built-in function named reversed:

```
nums = [2, 4, 6, 8]
# Print last element to first (zero index) element
for i in reversed(nums):
    print(nums[i])
```

The use of reverse is actually more efficient than the version that uses range and len. The reversed expression creates an object which can be iterated that enables the for the statement to traverse the elements of the list in reverse. The expression reversed(nums) has no effect on the contents of the list nums. It simply enables a backward traversal of the elements. The reversed function returns a generator that works like the following:

```
def my_reversed(lst):
""" Generate the elements of list lst from back to front.
   Works like the built-in reversed generator function.
"""
for i in range(len(lst) - 1, -1, -1):
    yield(lst[i])
```

Within the range expression, the first argument, len(lst) - 1, is the index of the last element in the list.

'lst'. The second argument, -1, indicates -1 terminates, but is not included in the range. The last argument -1 reflects the range counts backwards. Taken all together we see that the range spans the indices of all elements in the list, from the last to the first.

The reversed function is found in the _ _builtins_ _ module. The use of it requires no special import statement.

Summary of List Creation Techniques

A variety of ways to create lists in Python are known to programmers. The following lists have a good recap of all the list kinds learnt:

For example   [2, 4, 6, 8, 10, 12, 14, 16, 18, 20]

Literal Enumeration:

```
L = [2, 4, 6, 8, 10, 12, 14, 16, 18, 20]
```

Piecemeal Assembly:

```
L = [ ]
for i in range(2, 21, 2):
L += [ i ]
L = [2, 4, 6, 8, 10, 12, 14, 16, 18, 20]
```

Creation from a Generator or Range Expression:

```
L = list(range(2, 21, 2))
```

List Comprehension:

```
L = [x for x in range(1, 21) if x % 2 == 0]
```

Combination of Methods with List Concatenation:

```
L = list(range(2, 9, 2)) + [10, 12, 14] + [x for x in range(16, 21, 2)]
```

Lists vs. Generators

The two ways of expressing a sequence of values are known to us: generators and lists. What are the similarities between a list and generator?

Generators and lists have the following similar characteristics:

- Both the lists and generators represent a sequence of values. The order of the values matters a lot. A sequence contains first element and last element. In a sequence, every element has a predecessor except for the first element. Every element in the sequence has a successor except for last element.
- Both the generators and lists can be iterated by using the "for statement".

How are generators and lists different from each other? Both the lists and generators differ in the following ways:

- The elements in a list persist for the life of list, but the elements produced by a generator become available in turn as the iteration with the generator progresses. Previous elements are unavailable from that particular generator object once the iteration moves on from the current element.
- Generally, the memory required for a list will be greater than that for a generator that can produce the same sequence of values. This is

due to the reason that the generator manages only one element at a time, while a list must store all the elements in the sequence at the same time.

- Lists provide random access support, which means that any value at any position in the list is available at any time or you can say that it shows all-time availability. On the other hand, a generator serves up values one at a time, in order from the first to the last. The ith element cannot be obtained from a generator without first requesting all the elements that come before it.

- Lists provide support of forward and backward traversal. Generators can only provide support of forward traversal.

If random access is necessary for the sequence of values creation, a generator may be the better choice. The generator's sequence acts like a lazy list; it means that the sequence element exists only at the time when it is needed. On the other hand, if it is necessary for a program to have access to all the values of a sequence available at any time during the execution of the program, then the best choice is the list.

Unlike generators, a list must be fully populated with all of its elements before it truly is useful to the program.

Why do we use DJANGO for Python?

Django is an open-source web framework for Python which is used for quick web application development. It maintains, designs, and secures websites and help developers to develop websites with simplicity and flexibility. Django web framework is a toolkit of all the components needed for development. The main purpose of using Django web framework is actually its support in developing new applications instead of wasting time on already developed components. Django is full of useful features which is better than other web framework.

Easy to use

The use of Django web framework for Python is super simple and easy and is widely used as it is free and open-source. This open-source organization is maintained by a vast community of developers. Beginners, intermediates can learn about it through web searching, and even experts can get updated with newly added features and available versions by using Google and other search engines.

Application development

Django framework was developed by the online news operation team. The aim of this team was to use the Django for web application development by using the Python programming language to make it easier for programmers to use it. Django has libraries, templates, and APIS which work together. Cost minimization can be applied when using Django, which enable developers to upgrade developed applications with minimal cost. Changes and additions with Django result in super-fast development.

Operating System Development

Django web framework runs on any operating system, including Windows, Linux, and Mac, etc. It provides ORM with the help of which developers can easily migrate or move applications to other databases with few lines of code change. It acts as a layer between the developer and the database.

Documentation

Django has excellent documentation for its framework to develop different kinds of real-world applications. Other web frameworks use an alphabetical list of attributes, modules, and methods. Fresh learners who are learning for the first time can learn about this framework very easily due to its excellent documentation. It was also a difficult task for Django to develop and maintain the documentation quality, and it is one of the best open-source documentation.

Reliable and Scalable

Django is a well-maintained framework and is most likely used in the industry. Cloud providers are taking all measures to provide the best services to run Django applications easily and quickly on cloud platforms. Django developers are working in the same development for a long time, so they are getting strong hands on these areas to make them more efficient and functional.

Community Support

Django has one of the best open-source communities out there governed by the Django software foundation. It follows some rules like for events there is a code of conduct. Developers are connected to work on projects and solve the errors and other complexities if any. Django is more stable, offer packages, and has excellent documentation and good community support.

Main features and Users

The main features of Django are as follow:

- Model layers and Python compatibility
- Security
- Localization and optimization
- Geographic framework with common tools for development

- Template layers
- Forms
- Other core functionalities.

Django can be used to develop any kind of websites like content management system, social networking applications, Wiki-pages, chat applications, and other websites. Django works with multiple server-client applications and delivers content in any form, including HTML, JSON, XML, RSS, etc. Django is versatile and allows developers to focus on business logic and not on common utilities because Django does it for us. Choosing Django is a good choice of developers to complete website and application development in a short time with full protection from threats.

How Beneficial is DJANGO for the Existing Python Developers?

Python as a robust server-side programming language making it super simple for developers to develop websites of high performance immediately and quickly. Django is the most popular framework for Python is used for web development. Python encourages Django development packages and modules. Developers can easily distribute the code into different modules and reuse these modules over different projects. It is a great opportunity for developers to reduce the development time and complete a project quickly. Many other web frameworks are also used for Python, but among them, Django is more beneficial for developers to build high-quality web applications.

Benefits of Django

There are many benefits of Django for developers due to which it is the most popular web framework and mostly liked by developers. Here are some of them discussed below.

Precise Cleaner Code

The long-term advantages of a shorter and cleaner codebase means a lot to Python developers. Python allows developers to express common ideas and concepts with less code. At the same time, Django maintains MVC (Model-view-controller) pattern. This pattern helps the developers to fix their code efficiently by keeping the business logic, user interface, and application data separate. With the contributions of both Python and Django help developers to enjoy a readable, shorter, and cleaner code.

Web Application Customization

In the competitive world, each business wants to represent a website with a distinct and rich user experience. Developers need multiple options to customize a website without putting any extra efforts and time. Django provides such flexibility that enables developers to use multiple options in order to develop a great piece. Developers need not worry about full development but need focus on customization only. According to the client's requirements and specific needs, a developer needs to focus on website customization, and Django plays a key role to save the time of a developer.

Built-in Tools

Django updates bring new features in order to make it easier for developers creating a catchy piece. Django includes a variety of built-in tools with which common web developments tasks can be accomplished without writing lengthy codes. The built-in tools help developers up to a great extent, especially in heavy tasks and big projects.

Variety Packages

By using Django packages, developers find it useful and helpful in website creation. The performance of creating a website can be boosted by availing these packages. The packages include reusable tools, sites, and apps. Many developers like to use these apps frequently, such as using the Django extension, Django Celery, South, and Django Rest Framework. Developers emphasize the use of Django SHOP, Satchmo, matchless or Catridge, and Django-oscar to effectuate the development of e-commerce websites. Developers can also use other reusable tools, sites, and apps according to their needs. So, the use of these packages boosts website performance up to a great extent, which is why Django is of great importance and beneficial for developers.

Object-Relational Mapper (ORM)

Developers who are experienced in development prefer to use the object-relational mapper to write database queries without using SQL. However, the client-to-client needs result in different choices of the database. There is no need to write lengthy SQL queries only if the object-relational mapper is used to manipulate the database. The ORM is already implemented by default to allow developers to describe the database layout as a Python class. It also enables developers to access data in a more efficient way by using Python API, which is the available option. The API generates on the fly that does not require a developer to generate any additional code. Due to such functionalities, Django is widely used for data-driven websites.

Admin Interface

The client's requirements include a simple and dynamic interface for the smooth management of applications. The Django framework is designed with features and functionalities to generate a production-ready admin interface. The dynamic admin interface allows a user to add, change, and delete objects. It makes it super simple for a business to alter website content without using any backend interface. Developers take advantage of such features to run and setup admin sites while developing models.

Security Optimization

Python offers the best security optimization support, which cannot be found in any other programming language. In Django development, developers are also protected with the best security optimization support to optimize the security of web applications based on Python. Django is a unique web framework, generates web pages dynamically, and sends content to the web browser through templates, which is useful because the source code hides from both the browser and end-users. Due to this, the internet application gets comprehensive security cover. Developers can also use this to prevent cross-site scripting attacks, other security threats, and SQL injection.

Java maintained the first position in the world's ranking while Python stood third according to TIOBE index 2017. However, the recent report reflects a drastic increase in the usage of Python. The faster growth of Python indicates that Python has the ability to clinch the first place, but it may happen after the release of its version 4. Since 2016, Java has been in a heavy downward trend and may lose its position as long as Python continues such speed.

The decline of Java does not represent lacking in its usage, but it is due to the increase in the usage of Python language. However, Java is not going anywhere soon. According to a popular technology survey site, the latest usage statistics show that Java is being used by 3.0% websites as a server-side programming language while only 0.2% of websites use Python language.

Uptrend of Python

The latest TIOBE index indicates that Python is currently among the top three most popular programming languages, and it might jump to the 1st position in the near future. Another index shown by IEEE and its report is of great importance in the world with strong predictions based on the report. The following ranking is based on the usage of these languages in web application development on mobile devices, for enterprise, scientific applications, desktop, and the one used to program device controllers.

Differences between Java and Python

It is essential for developers to understand the differences between Java and Python.

Both Java and Python are high-level programming languages used for general purpose. Java is a statically typed language which needs a programmer to declare a variable before using it. On the other hand, Python gives a free hand to programmers to use variables without any declaration.

Java has lengthy codes, and programmers get tired to complete coding and accomplish a specific task. Programmers take extra time and use efforts to organize, maintain, and update Java codebase. On the other hand, Python enables programmers to enjoy coding with syntax simplicity and other functionalities, including built-in functions and many more, which enable programmers to express huge concepts in shortcodes. It brings easiness for a programmer to maintain and update codebases.

Java makes it easier for a programmer to create portable, cross-platform applications. These applications can run on any device on which the JVM is running. The JVM when is installed on devices then developers can run Java applications on many devices without requiring any compiler or specialized tools. On the other hand, Python developers need a compiler to convert the written code understandable by the specific operating system.

Java 8 can be used by programmers to avail its new features. The features include Lambda expressions, a new data API, and a new functional interface. Java programmers find it easy to switch from version 7 to 8 without facing any difficulty. On the other hand, Python versions are different from each other, specifically version 2 and 3. Switching from version 2 to 3 of Python is found to be challenging for programmers.

The speed and performance of Python and Java are different. Programmers have proved that Java is better than Python in speed and performance. Developers need to optimize the execution speed and performance of Python by using other tools, but the speed of Java can be optimized without using any tools.

Java is a popular web technology is also used for the development of applications for mobile operating systems i.e., Android. The Android SDK includes numerous standard libraries. Developers take advantage of networking, graphics, data structures, and math libraries. With this advantage, they can easily develop Android applications. Support for different tools and frameworks can also be taken in order to speed up the development. On the other hand, Python language cannot be used directly for the development of mobile applications. Additional frameworks and other tools are needed to use for mobile application development. Programmers prefer to use Java in order to save time and efforts.

Despite the lead of Java over Python somewhere, Python is a growing language due to its numerous applications and contributions. Python is the first choice of all the trending technologies in IT and is a great of programmers that become the reason for its huge surge in the number of users' year over year. Python was decided as the best choice for all the domains in IT which include infrastructure automation, web development, software testing, Big Data, and data science, etc. If the current trend of Python language continues, it will become the most sought language and overtake the number of jobs in the next years.

Python and Ruby are two of the most popular high-level programming languages which are dynamic scripting languages with the support of Object-Oriented Programming. Both Python and Ruby are the most powerful languages having interactive shell and collection of libraries. Support of both the languages in web development is of great importance and developers use the frameworks with great interest. However, both the languages have some difference which enables developers to select a better choice.

Ruby

Ruby is a high-level programming language designed by a Japanese computer scientist in 1995. Ruby is a dynamical type, scripting language, object-oriented and a reflective, general-purpose language. The philosophy of Ruby language does not include the only emphasis on how it runs best on a machine but also on making it user-friendly for developers to have fun using it. It is written in an elegant manner which is helpful and causes the least confusion for developers. Ruby supports both the procedural and functional programming, which means that it is a multi-paradigm programming language. The syntax of Ruby language is somewhat similar to that of Perl and Python language but with a strong influence of its object-oriented architecture. Vast community support is built around Ruby languages like Python and other programming languages. Ruby has IDEs built for practice just as Python has some built for developers to code. Ruby is also an open-source organization just as Python language with the biggest support of its frameworks. Its famous framework is Ruby on Rails which has popularized the language up to a great extent. After its release in 2005, it has been used in the development of websites such as Groupon and Twitter.

Similarities between Python and Ruby

The similarities between Python language and Ruby language are as follow:

- Python is available under the FSF-approved license while the Ruby is available under the OSI-approved license but the most interesting is that the developers need not to pay any license fee in order to use the two software or distribute them.
- Both of these languages are cross-platforms which mean that there are no specific operating system requirements and can run on both the Windows and Linux.
- No need to compile the programs of any of these two languages because they are high-level scripting languages.

- Python and Ruby both are dynamically types which allow programmers to use any variable without declaring it first.
- Python and Ruby programming languages support object-oriented programming (OOP)
- Python and Ruby both are available via Lambda functions at Amazon web services.

Differences between Ruby and Python

Python and Ruby programming languages are different in many ways. Here are some of the differences discussed below:

Use Cases

Ruby language is common in organizations for web application development. Ruby on Rails is a framework that allows for rapid development, and business teams focus on other business processes instead of coding functions from scratch. This framework provides a separator known as MVC structure (Model-view-controller). The MVC provides support in separating data, user interface, and business functions.

On the other hand, Python has the most popular MVC frameworks known as Django web framework for web application development. In addition, Python is also famous beyond the domains of web applications. For example, the Pandas library is useful for data preparation. Other libraries such as numpy and stats-model are also supportive in this case. Matplotlib is a powerful Python library for data visualization. Tensorflow is popular for machine learning tasks and projects. Besides, SciPy is another open-source library for Python, which is used for scientific computing and solving math functions that used to make engineering students sweat.

Flexibility

About Ruby, it follows the same approach as Perl follows. There is always another way to perform a task when it comes to Ruby and Perl, which is a similar philosophy in both. So, developers can find perform a task in many ways in ruby, depending on the developer's mind. This might lead to unnecessary complexity and confusion.

On the other hand, Python approaches to simplicity and complexity are removed by simplicity. Python has a different philosophy that is the problem solving is possible only in one way, and there is no another way to do it. The flexibility of Python language is reflected more by its code readability and simplicity. There is no need to follow another approach to solving the same problems while having one possible solution, which is super simple.

Popularity

The popularity of both languages is completely different from each other. The performance of Ruby language is getting slower with the passage of time in comparison to other languages. It shifted from the fifth position to the 10th in 2018 while the Python language has successfully achieved the 3rd position right now and steadily going up. It is also possible for Python to achieve the 1st place after the arrival of version 4 in 2022.

On the basis of job offers, stack overflow returns twice as many results when searching for Python instead of Ruby. Python leads by 20% over Ruby when it comes to LinkedIn. Almost all the job searches regarding development or programming include Python language as the first requirement. The salary of a Python programming is also high in comparison to other languages. However, Ruby developers have a better salary range at PayScale in the US market.

Code Reusability

Publically available code is a relevant factor when it comes to the decision of choosing the best programming language. Python has numerous modules which are available via PyPI, where more than 150000 modules can be searched. On the other end, the reusable code in Ruby is called Gems which are also touching the 150000 figure. The differentiating factor is the additional support of

Python PyPI, allows filtering by categories like "development status." It is straightforward, and its performance is better than comparing libraries and manual code evaluation.

Learning curve

The learning curve is bent towards Python language because it is easy to learn due to its simplicity, especially its syntax is easier to understand. Due to its readability, the process of learning Python from the beginning level to advance becomes quicker. On the other hand, Ruby language is not easy to understand and takes long for a beginner to absorb this language. Its syntax is not much difficult, but Python has more simple syntax as compared to that of Ruby.

When it comes to testing and troubleshooting, both the Python and Ruby languages have capable toolsets. An operator needs to recognize that reading errors is more evident than the unforgiving stack traces in Ruby.

Comparison Base	Ruby	Python
Core areas	The core areas include web development and functional programming	It includes scientific and academic programming with enormous libraries for data science
Use cases	Implementation of applications and high-traffic sites is quickly	Heavy-data sites and servers with high-traffic volume. Faster operating with big data, scientific calculations and math. Preferred for data analysis and prototyping
Motivation	Provide flexibility and freedom to get things done in myriad ways "Achieve more with less"	Emphasis on simplicity over flexibility "One right way to achieve things"
Properties	Efficient, powerful, expressive and elegant	Easy to learn, fast and simple, flexible, readable code
Propensity of Developers	Frequent updates, creative coding and readable code	Conservative code, fewer updates, and stable
Major application	Hulu, Twitter, Github and Airbnb	Spotify, YouTube, BitTorrent, Reddit and Instagram

Both Python and Ruby are super-fast languages of large and loyal community. Obviously, Python is the most preferred choice by data scientists for data analysis and prototyping. Both the Python and Ruby have powerful web frameworks, Ruby has Rails while Python has Django, but Django with few more of Python are mostly used for web development with the ease of learning Python.

Selection for backend development is always a tough job because both the PHP and Python are doing extremely well. Python is going in the uptrend and is going popular for web development. Most of the websites are programmed in PHP due to its features but nowadays; the frequent increase in the demand of Python for web development is recorded.

Performance of Python

According to the ranking of Datanyze, Python was dominating in the month of November 2018. The performance of PHP went down, and the graph of Python language is going in the uptrend. This uptrend reflects the increasing number of website development showing the interest of developers in Python programming language. Since PHP was dominating over the years, but now the trend is downward. It will not be an exaggeration if we say that Python language is an alternative language to the PHP in web development.

According to Stack Overflow, the use of Python programming language has been increasing in the US and UK by 27%, year to year growth. This growth is much higher than the growth of PHP.

There may be numerous reasons that need the attention of a programmer before selecting any language over another. In this case, the preference of Python over PHP decision is also a tough decision, and developers need to have a look at some of the reasons before making any decision. The following comparison will reflect why Python programming language may be a better choice for development.

Python vs. PHP

PHP has enjoyed a lot over the years as the most preferred language, but the upward trend of Python seems a little bit disruption for the PHP by covering most of the market. Here are some of the reasons the developers need to understand.

Well thought out Design

It looks friendly and easy to write code in Python than in PHP because the design of Python is well-thought-out as compared to that of the PHP. The Python architecture has shown full efforts to make it user-friendly when they code. On the other hand, PHP is not of a well-thought-out-design as compared to the Python.

Python wins in the ease of learning: Learning Python programming language is much easier than learning the PHP. It is difficult for a beginner to have a grasp over the PHP, but there is no issue in learning Python since it is known as the easiest language to learn. However, a professional programmer who has a grasp over multiple languages can easily deal with both Python and PHP. IDEs of the languages are available regardless of which type of operating system a developer uses. Learners can work on these IDEs, which are built with featured software. Furthermore, the open-source communities, as well as the learning material of Python, is easily accessible, that is one of the reasons why fresh learners are going towards Python.

Superior Framework

In the race of frameworks, Python programming language has superior frameworks than those of the PHP. The frameworks of Python are super simple and easily available, especially the Django web framework. Web development with Django web framework is super simple and easier than doing it with any other framework even those of the PHP. Developers always have choices depending upon several factors. Among the included factors, the standard is the one that is one of the causes of attraction and compelling use.

Python provides much convenience with its frameworks, including Django, Flask, Bottle, Pyramid, and Tornado. On the other end, the convenient PHP frameworks include Symphony, Kohana, Zend, and CodeIgniter.

As far as Python web frameworks are considered, Django is the clear winner with a larger number of users. It is a super-fast web framework and easy to use as compared any other web framework irrespective of any programming language. Due to its easy setup and shorter development time Django is preferred by developers.

The learning curve has bent to the frameworks than the languages. The deeper and richer is the framework the more learning areas are available. There is an upfront cost of web frameworks, but its benefit is in the long term.

More Readability

PHP follows a classic approach and is extensively documented. On the other hand, Python has strict use of indentation enforcement. On the basis of readability, Python does not beat PHP only but all the other programming languages as well.

Syntax Simplicity

The syntax of Python language is simple and much easier as compared to that of PHP. The code is easy to write and understand when it comes to Python language. The use of special characters reduces the development speed of a programmer when it comes to PHP, but Python makes it friction-less for a developer that is making it a more preferred choice.

Debugging Tools

Python has easily available debugging tools as it is a big developer ecosystem. The tools other than the debugging tools can also be utilized for different purposes. Python debugger (PDB) is a powerful debugger that is easy to use and well-documented.

On the other hand, PHP also has to debug support, and the debugger is known as XDebug. Python wins when it comes to debugging tools in comparison with that of PHP. Python requires fewer debugging tools than PHP.

Package Management

Python is a clear winner in package management as it acts as the glue between various projects. With the help of package management, packages can be written, built, and shared in such a format that can easily plug into other applications.

Package management also exists in PHP, but there is not any codebase using it to the extent that PIP does. PIP is a tool used for the installation and management of Python packages. It enables a developer to install, uninstall, upgrade, and use a broad range of sources, external and internal libraries.

Advantage of Python over PHP

Lambda keyword is used to create anonymous functions and is commonly known as Lambda function or a subroutine. It is actually a code block that can be passed around and executed later either once or maybe several time. The Lambdas work freely within Python and are super simple to create. Lambdas are used by developers when in need depending upon the task.

Earlier in PHP, there was only a "create_function" available which was not really a substitute for the Lambdas. Some changes have been done in the subsequent versions of the PHP, and now closure support is available.

Versatility

Python programming language is more versatile than the PHP, which is indicated by what these languages do and which one has the best performance. Python does more than website development that includes machine learning NLP, image processing, data science, website and mobile application development, and many more.

On the other hand, PHP may be used for several other purposes, but it is intended precisely for web page creation, and that is all it does the best. PHP is a programming language that is meant for creating sophisticated web programs.

Larger Community Support

Python is known to be an open-source organization, and a vast community is built around it. Since Python is used for multiple purposes and an enormous community is developing it much more. Every foundation like the Python Software Foundation expects even a larger community and better support.

The PHP programming language also has vast community support around it, but in comparison to the Python language, it still needs to fight in order to beat Python, but it seems impossible.

In the end, a developer looks for simplicity and adaptability, which results in the super-fast learning experience as well as it is difficult to go wrong. A programmer with such programming language can achieve programming goals efficiently.

The term PERL stands for Practical Extraction and Reporting Language. It was originally developed by Larry Wall in 1987, a system designed for reading, extracting, processing, collating and summarizing information from the logs and other data files. PERL is an excellent took for processing data, from the simple data collection and formatting information from the text files to the processing and generation of HTML and web forms.

No doubt that PERL is one of the most functionally rich languages, but there has been a move to replace the built-in functions with external modules and mostly object-based. However, PERL still includes the built-in functions for networking, file access, interpersonal communication, and interfacing to some of the core Unix system.

PERL is also an open-source language in order to facilitate the reporting processes, but its contribution is not that much of the communities built by Python and other programming languages. Neither the PERL community has many contributions nor much larger as compared to other high-level programming languages. However, PERL programming language has a contribution in various areas such as developing administrative systems, network programming, programs requiring graphics, and other applications.

PERL is one of the high-level dynamic languages which also support object-oriented programming. There is no restriction for the object system that is optional rather than compulsory part of the language. PERL is no doubt the best choice for specific tasks, but Python programming language provides strong support almost in all the projects related to programming. Migration from PERL to Python is a very good idea in order to get hands-on those projects which cannot be done with PERL language, but Python language helps with such projects.

PERL is neither the only language nor always the right language. A programmer must learn multiple programming languages in order to have a grasp over solving many different problems. Since using a programming language depends upon the task or project or finding possible solutions for a specific problem. Neither PERL can perform all the tasks nor any other programming language, but Python programming language has the best possible approach to solve any problem that is either simple or complex.

Disadvantages of PERL

Different languages have different weaknesses and strengths. PERL is not as popular as Python, Java, C, Javacscript and few others due to some reasons which are the cons of PERL language.

Following are the disadvantages of PERL:

- If programmer is going to write a Linux kernel code then PERL is a wrong choice. PERL is not suitable for such task that is the reason learning Python or other programming languages are necessary for complete programming.
- Prototyping a GUI application with PERL is a slowest way ever.
- PERL is not good for word processing and spreadsheets.
- Unreadable code or untidy code which is difficult to read the PERL codes
- No well implementation when it comes to Object-oriented programming with PERL
- PERL is slower for a lot of tasks when it comes to scripting
- PERL language is not portable
- It has not interpreter shell
- This language creates trouble when the code gets lengthier
- Libraries are not much appreciable
- Its argument handling is poor

Difficult to fix Bugs

Whenever any bug occurs, it is very difficult for PERL to fix the bug as compared to other programming languages. There is text causing difficulties for programmers to find bugs which is one of the disadvantages of PERL language.

Bad Choice for Web Programming

PERL is a bad choice when it comes to website development or application development. Therefore, the PERL language has no improved functionalities, scalability, speed and convenience for users.

The comparison of PERL language with Python programming language is not fruitful because both the languages have great contributions but Python programming language is preferred in most of the cases due to its features and performance almost in all the programming projects either simple or complex.

Python Programming Language is Considered Better than Other Languages

If we go through the market details, we have so many programming languages available and have been used in companies today. However, among these programming languages, Python is a high-level programing language. The structure of this language is well suited for many purposes and enables developers and programmers to express important concepts and necessary information in few and lesser words as compared to Java and C++. Python has the ability to support structured programming as well as to object-oriented programming. The language could also be incorporated into existing applications with requirements of programmable interface.

The Semantics of the Language

So the robust programing language Python is considered as greatly readable programing language. It is characterized and recognized by a visual layout which is uncultured and makes frequent and repeated use of English keywords. On the other hand, other programming languages make use of not English Keywords but use punctuation. Compared to the C language, it has a smaller number of syntactic exception.

Uses of Python in the Industry

Python is the popular programing language, especially in the web development field. Though predominantly and to a great extent used in the back end, it has great integration with database, good restatement time and some good number of web standards has been the reason of its fame in the industry. One of the famous question-answer platform Quora uses many python codes.

It is Python which is used to write applications with large size. A website like Google and NASA and YouTube make wide use of Python and specifically for its applications for smartphones. In addition, online transactions system in the US that is the New York Stock Exchange (NYSE). Some other ways and modes of using Python are:

1. Making of RSS reader
2. MySQL
3. Calendar creation in HTML
4. Working with files
5. Foe online applications, programing CGI

In addition, it is yet a famous tool that is widely used by software developers for testing and checking build control as well as management. Moreover, for task integration, Python is the language to be used by companies. We can take the example of 3D software Maya that makes use of Python for both complex integrations and for automating small user tasks.

Applications of Python

Languages like Python might not always be used to engender a unique product, but of course, it is used to power the tools which are responsible for the creation of such kind of products. For example, look at the companies with a smart internal system in use. They do not need compiled languages.

Moreover, the language has found diverse applications in companies that develop software and games, language development, web framework, and many more. This gives Python an edge over the rest of the programing languages, and that is the reason for its success in the industry. Let's dive into some of the advantages Python has in the industry.

- Provision of support for large standard libraries that are equipped with a number of operations like web service tools, internet, protocols, and operating system interfaces.
- It is also used to integrate EAI Enterprise Application Integration that makes it possible and convenient to pave the way of development of Web services like COBRA or COM components by invoking them. Its control capabilities are very powerful and call directly through C++, C, and Javascript via Jython.
- It yet processes XML and other languages because it can easily run

and operate on a modern system of operations using the same byte.

- It has the capabilities to improve programming productivity. The clear and object-oriented design has increased from two to ten-fold productivity of the programs while making use of languages like Perl, Java, C, and C++.

- The integration features are way too strong, and its unit testing and enhanced control abilities which results in increased speed for the productivity of most of the applications that use Python and the important thing is scalability which makes this language a great option for protocol network applications.

- In the current era, big data is becoming extensively important for big corporations, and especially when it comes to businesses. So, when it is about data processing, data scientists prefer to use Python as a tool for the operations. This is the sole reason that Python has become the best PL to be used when it comes to big data.

- So for building analytical tools, data scientists find Python the best fit. Moreover, since data is something that makes you money in the current era, the use of Python could not be ignored and should be incorporated in your execution plan.

- It is especially more desired for machine learning, and this is one of the leading businesses around the world right now. Advanced machine learning could be further used for a huge number of tasks in the business.
- Finally, we should be talking about the cybersecurity which is very important in the current digital era of the world where we have these money exchanges gone digital, and this is very important to have the cybersecurity very strong to reflect hacking attempts. According to a survey about the cybersecurity performance of Python, it is a clear winner in the industry right now.

In addition to all the aforementioned stuff, it is yet another great feature of the programing language that Python is completely free and you do not need to pay a penny for it. Moreover, from this, it means that the expansion set of supporting modules and tolls and libraries are free. A wide number of its integrated development environments are free like Eclips, Pydev, and PTVS and Spyder Python and more.

So these are some of the reasons which have made Python the best fit for businesses and in the industry. I thin without Python; these big tech giants would not have been so much able in terms of influence and of course, monetary power. It is going to give rise to the nest IoT boom in days to come and most importantly in machine learning.

The Reason Behind the Huge Demand of Python Developers

One might argue that the era of Python was just 2017 when it witnessed some great rise in the popularity and growth across the world. The recent However, according to statistics and data, the recent rise in the growth of Python could not be ignored.

However, why do you think it will keep on attaining the rise in the expansion and in size? To answer the question, we dive into the market data and the scale of Python adoption and acquisition by corporations and companies around the world.

SO the reason behind the popularity of Python is one and simple. It will be as popular and widely used five years from now as it was five years ago. This is a big statement and to prove this, we need to see in detail what makes Python so special for these developers and programmers.

Years ago, when Python came into the market, people believed it would be dead within months of inception. In face when Larry Wall who is also the founder and brain behind programing language Perl was delivering his third annual state of Pearl Opinion said that there are some programming languages out there in the market that are C++, Java, Perl, Visual Basics, Javascript and in the last Python. Back then, the leading language for programming was C++ and Perl was on the third number in the market. Python had very low demand and was not included among the PLs that could grow.

However, in the years to follow, Python grew with tremendous speed and outshined Perl as well. According to Stack Overflow, the visitor volume to question and enquire about Python increased more rapidly than Perl.

Following are the reasons behind the rise and super demand for Python among developers.

Data Science

This is one of the most adored languages among data scientists, unlike R and C++. SO the current era is the era of big data, and since Python supports large sets of libraries, internet, and prototypes, Python is the best and fully suited language for the operations. PyMySQL, PyBrain, and NumPy are the reason why is Python so extensively demanded. In addition, integrations and programming are the things a programmer has to deal in everyday life, and this is the reason behind the huge demand for Python as well because it provides easy integration even of existing apps or sites to other programming languages. This makes it future-oriented and scalable.

Machine Learning

In the industry these days, artificial intelligence and machine learning have created a huge buzz with every industry investing in the areas to maximize their revenue and cut costs. This is not really possible without the induction of Python. It is actually an interpreted language, and its use makes it elucidated enough to be interpreted by machines and to be understood by the hardware. The growth of ML has been on the rise in the last few years, and I think this is also one of the reasons why Python has witnessed a surge in its demand.

Applications in Web Development

According to data, Python is chosen by two out of three developers who in the start worked with OHO, and this is an achievement. The rising trend of Python in the last couple of years shows that it seems like the best alternative. It offers Flask and Django, which makes the process of web development easy and quick. It is due to these reasons and features that leading tech giants like Google, Facebook, Instagram, etc. have been using it for long. Uber and Google use it for its algorithms. In addition, it is super simple, and this is the reason why it is easy to work with and adaptable.

Automation

Automation is the need of the current era, and with Python, you can automate tasks by writing test scripts, and Python surprises you here as well. You need a very little number of lines required to automate. This is because it supports lots of modules and tools, making stuff easy and instant.

Multipurpose

It is like the Swiss Army Knife, which would be used for many purposes. Python is not just a thing that deals with discipline but supports all sources of data like data from SQL or MongoDB. API of Python, which is called PySpark, is used to distribute computing. It has an inbuilt feature of service provision for natural language processing NLTK.

- Python also has many applications in the provision of services for internet protocol like XML, LSON, and HTML.
- Python enables you to draft a user interface for applications already made. To do this, there are tool kits available which are wxWidgets, Kivy which is for writing multi-touch applications and finally QT via PySide.
- It provides great applications for the scientific community like SciPy, which

is a package for mathematics, engineering, and science. Pandas is a modeling and data analysis library.

- Python is extremely powerful when it comes to editing and works session recordings.
- Examples of software development applications are SCons, which is for build control, Roundup, and Trace, which are for bug tracking and project management. For IDE integrated development environments, Roster is used.
- The most important stuff related to Python is that it provides special applications for education.
- Its applications in business include Tryton, which is a 3-tier and advanced level application platform. Another management software called Odoocomes with a huge deal of business applications. This actually makes Python an all-rounder.
- For network programming, we have Twisted Python which provides a platform and framework for the network programming that is asynchronous. It has a simple socket interface.
- We all know that the gaming industry is evolving with great potential and ability to create replicated amount of revenue. The applications of Python

for gaming is very safe to use and have been pretty much and widely used. PyGame and PyKyra are bi-development frameworks for games. There is also a variety of 3D rendering options in the libraries.

- Moreover, we have applications which interest the developers to a huge extent and are used widely. We have applications that are console-based, applications for robotics, machine learning and web scraping and scripting and whatnot.

These are the main reason why Python is the best fit in the industry from the point of view of a developer.

According to a report of myTectra, the jobs which were posted in Naukri from 2014 to 2017 have been monitored. The trend of Python jobs is compared to the world's number one language showing different results.

Language	April 2014	April 2015	April 2016	April 2017
Java jobs postings	17000+	17000+	15000+	12000+
Python jobs postings	200+	500+	2500+	6500+

The graph shows that the increasing numbers of Python developers create worries for Java developers. However, the competition in the market is too much strong, and developers need to decide the best fit for future use. Python is no doubt a big challenge for all the other programming languages and competition with Python is now almost impossible for other languages.